Palgrave Studies in Family Business Heterogeneity

Series Editors
Esra Memili, University of North Carolina at Greensboro,
Greensboro, NC, USA
Erick P. C. Chang, Griffin College of Business, Arkansas
State University, Jonesboro, AR, USA

Contemporary family business research has been moving from highlighting the differences between family and non-family firms to the differences among family firms owing to the financial and non-financial dynamics that influences the strategic decisions and family firm actions. While a prominent stream of research draws attention to financial and non-financial goals (such as socioemotional wealth preservation) and other factors, we still do not know enough about such idiosyncrasies. This series will take a closer look at both financial and non-financial family firm idiosyncrasies across the globe and consider the ecosystem (i.e., regulatory framework, values, culture, access to finance, markets, R&D, and technology), and other national and economic conditions that allow the operations and presence of family firms.

Editors
Esra Memili, UNC Greensboro
Erick P. C. Chang, Arkansas State

Editorial Board
Ernesto J. Poza, Arizona State University

Carol B. Wittmeyer, St. Bonaventure University
Jim Cater, University of Texas at Tyler

More information about this series at
http://www.palgrave.com/gp/series/16464

Claudio G. Müller ·
Fernando Sandoval-Arzaga

Family Business Heterogeneity in Latin America

A Historical Perspective

Claudio G. Müller
School of Economics and Business
University of Chile
Santiago, Chile

Fernando Sandoval-Arzaga
Tecnologico de Monterrey
Monterrey, Nuevo León, Mexico

ISSN 2662-6055 ISSN 2662-6063 (electronic)
Palgrave Studies in Family Business Heterogeneity
ISBN 978-3-030-78933-6 ISBN 978-3-030-78931-2 (eBook)
https://doi.org/10.1007/978-3-030-78931-2

This Palgrave Macmillan imprint is published by the registered company Springer Nature Switzerland AG
The registered company address is: Gewerbestrasse 11, 6330 Cham, Switzerland

Series Editors' Preface

A prominent stream of research has been drawing attention to the differences among family firms in terms of governance, financial and non-financial dynamics, and strategies. Using the extant research to date that includes the *Palgrave Handbook of Heterogeneity among Family Firms* as a point of departure, it is our distinct pleasure and honor to present the *Palgrave Studies in Family Business Heterogeneity.*

Our inaugural book focuses on the evolution of family firms throughout the Latin American region. Indeed, family firms interact with and are substantially influenced by their external environment (i.e., country and regional contexts). In turn, family firms also influence their external environment encompassing formal (e.g. economic, legal, and political) and informal institutions (e.g. norms, values, beliefs, and attitudes). Hence, in family firms, the decision to start a business and then venture management are led by both individual characteristics of firms and owners as well as the external environment in which firms operate.

Claudio Muller and Fernando Sandoval-Arzaga provide a historical perspective on more than five centuries of institutional changes and resource combinations that have paved the way for multiple entrepreneurial families to start and manage businesses with different scopes and goals shaped by regional forces in Latin America. In different sections of the book, the authors illustrate four distinctive waves where traditions have been transmitted over generations to develop a unique type of social capital that is highly idiosyncratic to the Latin American region. From the earlier entrepreneurs who arrived from Europe to seize the vast opportunities in the "New World" to the migration flows from other continents, each wave nurtures and blends with the next one to enrich it and endows family businesses the melting pot of which Latin American society represents today.

The primary enlightening aspect of the book is the diversity and different challenges each family business has endured over generations. The authors proficiently guide the readers about the emergence of a highly heterogeneous group of industry sectors through the integration of pre-Columbian products and services with the Western European technology which are endowed with traditions and familiness to make them competitive on a global scale.

We expect family business scholars and practitioners in general to find this book highly useful for gaining more understanding about the unique culturally rich region.

Esra Memili
Erick P. C. Chang

Acknowledgments

We would like to acknowledge and thank the eight families that inspired us in the writing of this book. Without their stories of legacy and entrepreneurship this book would not have had the practical vision we wanted to capture. Many of these families have origins dating back almost to the colonial period and other success stories are a bit more current, but no less important.

In addition, we would like to thank those with whom we have discussed the heterogeneity of family businesses in Latin America, some friends and colleagues who come from different sciences, such as anthropologists, historians, communication theorists and sociologists... without their valuable contributions we would not have been able to finish this text.

Likewise, we would like to acknowledge Esra Memili and Erick Chang for inviting and motivating us to be part of this Palgrave Studies in Family Business Heterogeneity series, but above all for their wise advice that helped us to improve the quality and rigor of this text, which we hope will be a contribution to family business research. We would also like to acknowledge the assistance and support of Marcus Ballenger and his team at Palgrave Macmillan, who allowed us to move this work forward diligently to see the book through from idea to publication.

Finally, we would like to thank our families, because we stole their time during this pandemic: Ivonne, Rai, and Ame as well as Guille, Fer, and Guillo. For us this is the biggest family business.

Praise for *Family Business Heterogeneity in Latin America*

"Family businesses in Latin America carry a series of stereotypes and one of them is that they are all small. This book introduces us to Latin American family businesses and the social and economic impacts far beyond the families that have owned and operated them. The heterogeneity of family businesses in Latin America forces us to study the importance of Latin America as a global player, but especially the fundamental role that family businesses in this region have played in the economic development of their countries during the last 500 years."

—Alfredo De Massis, *Professor of Entrepreneurship & Family Business, Free University of Bolzano, Italy; Lancaster University, United Kingdom and IMD, Switzerland*

"This important work gives us an opportunity to discover the origin of the admirably successful family legacies emerging from Latin America. Recognizing their history and culture and how these have evolved and shaped their present identities is key to realizing the important roles they are to play in the future of their countries. Acknowledging heterogeneity as alternately a source of adversity and a competitive advantage, the authors are taking us on a journey through time and are demonstrating the powerful role of multigenerational family enterprises in shaping Latin America's economies."

—Ramia El Agamy, *Editor-in-Chief of Tharawat Magazine,*
Host of The Family Business Voice

"Family Business Heterogeneity in Latin America is the book we have been needing, but not just for Latin America! Muller and Sandoval-Arzaga have done what we should all have been doing in studying families in business—They have documented how the larger social, legal, economic environments impact the formation and growth of family enterprises. All too often we treat these cases as though only the family and the business and perhaps the competition determine behavior. I hope scholars learn the lessons this book has to offer."

—Frank Hoy, *Beswick Professor of Innovation and Entrepreneurship,*
Foisie Business School, Worcester Polytechnic Institute, USA

"In this new book, professors Claudio Muller and Fernando Sandoval-Arzaga provide a much-needed in-depth investigation of the different types of family businesses that exist across Latin America. The particularly unique, and extremely valuable, historical approach that Muller and Sandoval-Arzaga offer open up many new paths through which we can better understand the role and importance of family businesses in this region of the world. The different chapters offer a plethora of perspectives that cast new light on how and why family businesses have played, and still play, a crucial role in the emergence and development of the economies in most Latin American countries. The book offers an excellent combination of history, theory and practical case studies that will make it valuable for scholars, students, and practitioners alike. I highly recommend this unique and ambitions book to anyone who has an interest in entrepreneurship, business history and family business in a Latin American context."

—Professor Mattias Nordqvist, *House of Innovation.*
Stockholm School of Economics, Sweden

"With over 7 million families of Italian descent in Argentina and the largest Japanese diaspora in Sao Paolo, Brazil outside of Japan, Latin America is a mosaic of varied cultures and communities that makes each region within the continent unique. Authors of this must-read book are to be complemented for bringing to life migratory flows and idiosyncratic fascinating journeys of families featured in it! A delightful thought-provoking reading!"

—Pramodita Sharma, *Schlesinger Grossman Chair of Family Business, Grossman School of Business, University of Vermont, USA*

Contents

List of Figures

List of Tables

1

Introduction

Latin America is a region of marked contrasts with different and varied economic, cultural, and political developments since the original peoples of the region and up to the very moment of its discovery and subsequent colonization process in 1492. With a population of more than 641 million inhabitants in 2018[1] (World Bank, 2020), the region represents about 13% of the world's land area. Its people share not only the majority Spanish language—with the exception of Brazil, where the language is Portuguese—and the Catholic Christian religion, but also the fact that many Migration flows have shaped different societies and countries in the region (Meade, 2016).

The promise of economic wealth in this land, initially called West Indies, motivated the arrival of millions of people from different regions of the world, especially across the Atlantic Ocean, which later gave way to the Conquest of America. This first period of extraction of gold, silver, and other precious metals led to a more permanent settlement of the first

---

[1] https://data.worldbank.org/indicator/SP.POP.TOTL.

© The Author(s), under exclusive license to Springer Nature Switzerland AG 2021
C. G. Müller and F. Sandoval-Arzaga, *Family Business Heterogeneity in Latin America*, Palgrave Studies in Family Business Heterogeneity, https://doi.org/10.1007/978-3-030-78931-2_1

settlers who saw this land as a new home. Huge Migration flows brought life to this region during its first 200 years.

Referring to the different movements to gain independence from Spain and Portugal, the colonial legacy was succeeded by the different independence processes of the Kingdom of Portugal and the Spanish Crown. Each of the different colonies began, in a singular way, to create a local society. By the middle of the eighteenth century, the centralized bureaucratic control that characterized Latin America bore its first fruits of emancipation.

The end of colonial domination marked the beginning of large commercial monopolies in Latin America. This coincided with a period of acute crisis of social revolutions and massive processes of social mobilization. In almost all countries, wars were prolonged, marking the life of the new rising states in Latin America (Bértola & Ocampo, 2012). This implied an almost natural selection of those families that were closer to the Viceroyalty system—responsible for administering and governing, on behalf of the Monarchies, a country or a province in America—, a system inherited from colonialism, and that later managed to adapt to the installation of the new independent republics that were created after 1810.

Along with the dynamics of Independence, nationalism, and the search for one's own identity, was nuanced by the different migration flows that converged during more than 200 years. One of these flows was the arrival of more than 12 million Africans across the Atlantic between 1492 and the mid-nineteenth century, which exceeded by four times the number of migrants arriving from Europe. This represents the largest mass movement of people in human history (Crawford & Campbell, 2012).

Another example is the arrival of migrants, who in many regions came to represent 35% of the population, as in the case of Uruguay at the end of the nineteenth century and 30% of the population of Argentina in a similar period. In sum, migrants and their descendants came to represent more than 70% of the entire population in South America. Given their demographic weight, they also had an enormous impact on the configuration of popular culture in the region. They diversified meat consumption and turned foods such as pasta and wine into national staples. They also introduced sports and leisure activities such as handball, polo, and soccer.

As these new societies formed, there was a convergence of both economic and political power, which was cradled for new family businesses in the region (Gomez-Mejia et al., 2020; Rautiainen et al., 2019). This mix resulted in a particular and unique family and organizational culture based on the new institutional conditions, providing abundant differences across the region.

From a macro perspective, Douglass North, with his Theory of Institutional Change (North, 1990), presents some principles that help to understand the legal and institutional factors that have affected this region and to understand that each society creates restrictions that limit political, economic, and social interactions. These include informal constraints, such as sanctions, customs, traditions, and codes of conduct, as well as formal rules: constitutions, laws, and property rights. Over the course of Latin American history, institutions evolved to create order and reduce market uncertainty. The diversity from the birth and founding of Latin American societies was also successful because of the way governments were creating and promoting their own rules of the game. The first families assimilated these rules of the game and adapted to the new conditions, particularly customs, traditions, and codes of conduct that were passed on from generation to generation.

Heterogeneity implies that firms have different resources and capabilities, and even that, with similar resources, they perform differently. The idiosyncratic variety of resources found in family businesses represents a vital determinant of their heterogeneity (Chua et al., 2012). Family business can develop unique competitive advantages due to the distinct resources that arise from family involvement and the development of social capital, survival capital, patient capital, and human capital (Habbershon & Williams, 1999).

Particularly social capital (Arregle et al., 2007) is identified as a competitive advantage for family businesses because it is the social capital of the family that is embedded in the social capital of the firm. In this way, the family's social capital was formed generation after generation. Like other forms of capital, social capital constitutes a form of accumulated history that reflects investments in social relations and social organization over time. Time is relevant to the development of social capital, since all forms of capital depend on the stability and continuity of the social structure. Together with social capital we must, from a historical point of view, add the cultural heritage of family businesses (Colli, 2003), i.e., the resources, competencies, identity, knowledge, and prestige that are transmitted intergenerationally.

A relevant component of our research has been to highlight the phenomenon of migration, which is defined as a change of permanent or semi-permanent residence. For most migrants it was a permanent change, in many cases it was also forced migration, as in the case of the cullies and slaves from Africa. Our analyses also explain that the volume of migration in Latin America varied in size and degree of diversity. In fact, we found a high degree of diversity in most of the subregions studied not limited to the geographical area, in other words, large geographical areas such as Brazil received a great heterogeneity of migrants in contrast to what happened with Argentina where it received a greater volume of migration but more homogeneous in its origin.

One of the pioneering studies to consider the concept of heterogeneity within family businesses was Moores and Mula (2000). These authors uncovered findings on differences in the management control system among a class of family businesses based on life-cycle stage, using markets and clans to provide the first empirical evidence of heterogeneity. This insight has inspired other studies in family business heterogeneity, albeit less incipiently to make room for contributions from historical, anthropological, and sociological perspectives (Muller et al., 2018).

The purpose of this book is to build on the framework of social capital and cultural heritage, institutional theory and organizational ambidexterity, an exemplification of the nuances of heterogeneity of family businesses in Latin America, as well as to showcase regions and firms that have not received the attention they deserve. This book examines how families form enterprises that survive across generations, influencing and being influenced by their local and regional environments. This text also wants to contribute to reflection and allow us to abandon stereotypes of family businesses if we really want to understand their complexity in emerging economies.

The difficulties experienced during the progress of this book were enormous because of the scarcity of sources, definitions, concepts, and methodologies appropriate to the analysis of the heterogeneity of family businesses in this region and on the other hand because many authors and researchers have uncritically applied concepts and theories that come from spaces with very different experiences of the Anglo-Saxon or Asian field. Breaking with the dominant theoretical paradigms of the Anglo-Saxon world, and openly debating how we can and how we should study business families and family-controlled businesses in our countries has been another objective of this book.

Another challenge has been to clearly establish certain definitions of the unit of study. Our analysis indicates that most experts in family business field tend to accept that there are three types of similar organizational forms: (1) family business, the way a business is legally independent where ownership and management is strategically controlled by one or more families for at least two generations. (2) family group, which corresponds to identifying the partial or total participation in the ownership of several legally independent companies in which the management by a family is strategically controlled and (3) business family, which is a concept that defines families with a degree of blood or spiritual kinship that over several generations have made productive investments in different businesses, whatever the case, the objective is to make the values and continuity of that family endure over time, through the firm.

One of the evidence that we show in this book is that the real protagonists of family-controlled businesses are, in this long-term approach, families, and not necessarily firms. Another important finding of the reflections of this book is that the organizational forms that families have adopted in the long term in Latin America is that they have been flexible to the environment, institutional, financial, market, and available technologies. The form of legally independent company, or business group, or are in this historical view a changing organizational component, adapted in their long-term strategies of family businesses. The essence of the largest business families in these territories has been, and is, the capacity and intention (achieved or failed) to recombine resources over time with the will to allow the family to survive in business, with the most efficient organizational format as appropriate to different external environments, and according to the variable internal evolution of the families.

This book is organized into five main sections, we start with a Theoretical Perspectives on Heterogeneity in Latin American Family Businesses, in this section we will present some of the approaches that seem relevant to us when addressing this historical perspective on the sources of heterogeneity of the family business by using theoretical frameworks from different perspectives ranging from economic aspects, sociology, and management. We do not pretend to offer an exhaustive literature review methodology, our objective is to present the theoretical frameworks used during the development of the text, based on the experience of the authors and many hours of conversation with different scholars from other areas of knowledge such as anthropology and sociology. Then we introduce the concept of waves. Chapter 3: The syncretism (The first wave), where we present the historical process of Latin American syncretism as a basis for the emergence of the first family businesses in the continent. In Chap. 4: First migration flows (The second wave) a new culture of family businesses, we identify the different processes of migration flows in different Latin American countries, linking them to the emergence of family businesses in the region. Chapter 5: Mapping the formation of the family group (The third wave): From state-owned companies to large family groups, develops a mapping of the emergence of large family groups as part of a process of industrialization and privatization in Latin America and their links with political power. Finally, Chap. 6: The new wave of global family entrepreneurs identifies the triggers for the success of a global entrepreneurial family as a new form of wealth creation in Latin America.

For each of the sections we present two cases of families, from Mexico to Patagonia in southern Chile, passing through Colombia, Brazil, and Argentina. There are eight stories of families that will inspire and show the heterogeneity of family businesses in the region. In this way, we want to represent the thousands of family businesses that have had a social and economic impact far beyond the families that have owned and operated them. The great sources of heterogeneity of family businesses in Latin America demonstrate the global importance of this region in the world and the fundamental role that family businesses have played in the economic development of their countries and regions.

This text is also a demonstration that the development of the discipline known as "family business" is still in a growth stage and is reflected in the fact that more and more scholars from other disciplines are approaching the study and practice of the different dimensions of this specialty.

Despite the limitations that this book may have, we think that this book will serve to discover the origin of the admirably successful family legacies that emerge from Latin America. Recognizing their history and heritage and how they have evolved and shaped their current identities is critical to realizing the important roles they must play in the future of their countries. Recognizing heterogeneity as alternatively a source of adversity and a competitive advantage, we invite readers to this journey through time. We want to demonstrate the powerful role of family businesses in shaping Latin American economies.

We invite researchers from all disciplines to overcome the necessary but not sufficient comparison that family businesses are different from non-family businesses and consider the extent to which family businesses act heterogeneously through empirical and anecdotal evidence.

References

Arregle, J. L., Hitt, M. A., Sirmon, D. G., & Very, P. (2007). The development of organizational social capital: Attributes of family firms. *Journal of Management Studies, 44*(1), 73–95.

Bértola, L., & Ocampo, J. A. (2012). *The economic development of Latin America since independence*. OUP Oxford.

Chua, J. H., Chrisman, J. J., Steier, L. P., & Rau, S. B. (2012). Sources of heterogeneity in family firms: An introduction.

Colli, A. (2003). *The history of family business, 1850–2000*. Cambridge University Press.

Crawford, M. H., & Campbell, B. C. (Eds.). (2012). *Causes and consequences of human migration: An evolutionary perspective*. Cambridge University Press.

Gomez-Mejia, L., Basco, R., Gonzalez, A. C., & Muller, C. G. (2020). Family business and local development in Iberoamerica. *Cross Cultural & Strategic Management*.

Habbershon, T. G., & Williams, M. L. (1999). A resource-based framework for assessing the strategic advantages of family firms. *Family Business Review, 12*(1), 1–25.

Meade, T. A. (2016). *History of modern Latin America: 1800 to the present*. Wiley.

Moores, K., & Mula, J. (2000). The salience of market, bureaucratic, and clan controls in the management of family firm transitions: Some tentative Australian evidence. *Family Business Review, 13*(2), 91–106.

Muller, C. G., Botero, I. C., Cruz, A. D., & Subramanian, R. (Eds.). (2018). *Family firms in Latin America*. Routledge.

North, D. C. (1990). *Institutions, institutional change and economic performance*. Cambridge University Press.

Rautiainen, M., Rosa, P., Pihkala, T., Parada, M. J., & Cruz, A. D. (2019). *The family business group phenomenon*. Springer International Publishing.

World Bank. (2020). Accessed April 2021 from https://databank.bancomundial.org/reports.aspx?source=2&country=LCN.

2

Theoretical Perspectives on Heterogeneity in Latin American Family Businesses

Unlike other regions of the world, family businesses in Latin America are relatively younger and have been able to adapt to the sociocultural, political, and market changes associated with independence process (1808–1890 years) and then globalization.

This was a heterogeneous process of evolution and transformation in many ways, especially if we compare it to the development of independence in the United States in 1787, where it was relatively diligent and quick to reach an agreement with the 55 representatives of the former colonies to draft a constitution and create a single federal government (Clinton, 1989). On the other hand, other regions, from Mexico to Argentina and Chile, experienced almost 100 years of complicated independence processes. This is illustrative of how similar groups had such different developments that, in this case, converged in the founding of the countries that constitute the Latin American region today.

Establishing the different theoretical perspectives on heterogeneity in family businesses in the region goes hand in hand with the context of the progress and evolution of this field. Research on family businesses has been a relatively recent academic area. Contrasting other disciplines,

© The Author(s), under exclusive license to Springer Nature
Switzerland AG 2021
C. G. Müller and F. Sandoval-Arzaga, *Family Business Heterogeneity
in Latin America*, Palgrave Studies in Family Business Heterogeneity,
https://doi.org/10.1007/978-3-030-78931-2_2

this subject was initially approached from practice and by family business professionals who first efforts, through observation and advice to family-owned and managed companies, were focused on articles based on the observation of certain overlapping phenomena and case studies (Donnelley, 1964). This area of research has been held back by several factors, including the lack of consensus on what constitutes a family business and the adoption of methodologies and theories, that adequately explains this overlap. A seminal paper by Worthman indicated that "no one really knows what the entire field is like or what its boundaries are or should be" (Worthman, 1994: 4). As a result, early published work has a more phenomenological approach than systematically exploring and advancing theoretical paradigms.

As in other world regions, early research on family business in Latin America focused on succession, family governance, performance, and other related issues (Parada et al., 2016). Nevertheless, none of the works have managed to identify critical variables and their interrelationships, leading to theoretical conceptualizations that rely on both generalities and cultures such as European or North American, without questioning the generalization coming from family business research in developed economies. What is more, the Latin American region has been significantly underrepresented in the number of scientific articles; indeed, if one looks at reputable journals, such as Family Business Review, only 8 of the 685 (about 1%) provide data from Latin America.[1]

A recent article by Miller and Le Breton-Miller (2021) entitled "Family Firms: A Breed of Extremes?" indicates that the literature on family firms has grown over the past two decades, but that much of the work has resulted in contradictory descriptions: family firms were outperformers or underachievers; outstanding innovators or archconservatives; negligent polluters or exemplary environmentalists. Numerous studies argue that this heterogeneity is due to differences in leadership, ownership, or family generations. Other studies found that the differences were due to context, whether governmental and legal frameworks, environmental uncertainties, institutional gaps, or even institutional

---

[1] Why Family Businesses are the Hidden Gems of Latin America. A Conversation with Prof. Claudio Müller. Tharawat Magazine by Ramia El Agamy Khan, 2018–07–13.

logic. Alternatively, they were due to the diversity of family goals and objectives: some families favor socioemotional benefits such as preservation of ownership control and intergenerational transfer, while others are more driven to seek short-term financial results (Gómez-Mejia et al., 2011).

The literature has highlighted that the most common organizational form globally is enormously heterogeneous, and it is a significant topic for research (Memili & Dibrell, 2019). Likewise, comprehending the evolution of historical patterns in a region such as Latin America is a challenge because of the unique interpretation and meaning that Latin American society places on the family as an institution and its relationship with economic activities. In fact, structural, psychosocial, and transactional family aspects play a more preponderant role in Latin America than in other regions of the world (Stangej & Basco, 2017).

In line with the above, Latin America is not a uniform region regarding its institutional context, whether formal or informal. This is given by differences in formal institutional quality, property rights, judicial systems, and corruption levels (Gomez-Mejia et al., 2020), as well as the informal institutional context, such as cultural and religious aspects, which require greater attention because they are the essence that binds the social and economic environment of family dynamics (Botero et al., 2019; Guajardo-Trevino, 2021).

In this section we will present some of the approaches that seem relevant to us when addressing this historical perspective on the sources of heterogeneity of the family business in Latin America by using theoretical frameworks from different perspectives ranging from economic aspects, sociology, and management.

2.1 Theoretical Perspectives

One of the characteristics of the field of family business is that different studies focus on investigating and knowledge the reasons, meanings, and dynamics in the interplay between family and business systems (Melin et al., 2014). Currently, more and more attention has been paid to the boundaries of the field, beyond the theories frequently used by a large part of researchers and scholars. Much of the family business literature has historically been tied to entrepreneurship because of its link to small businesses. However, more recent studies encompass a broader spectrum of interrelated fields linked by the fact that families as owners and managers may have an influence on a wide variety of firm activities and outcomes (Marjański & Sułkowski, 2020). Indeed, what we know about family firms is held in a vast array of theoretical lenses and perspectives, and it is difficult to identify and understand the distinctive nature of the field it has evolved from classical lenses to incorporate theories that are deeply rooted in social areas, sociology, or political economy.

While we do not pretend to offer an exhaustive literature review methodology, our objective is to present the theoretical frameworks used during the development of the text. As previously mentioned, the book has been divided into four main sections corresponding to the period before colonial emergence up to the present day. The following Table 2.1 presents a breakdown of these models used as theoretical support for the book.

Table 2.1 Theoretical approaches to the study of heterogeneity in family businesses in Latin America

Wave	Name	Theoretical organizational frameworks used in the book	
		Level of analysis	Approaches
First	The syncretism	Macro	Identity Theory for n-Culturals
Second	Migration flow	Macro	Lee's Theory
		Micro	Internal Social Capital
Thirty	Large family groups	Macro	Theory of Institutional Change
		Micro	Resource-based view
Fourth	Global entrepreneurs	Micro	Theory of Uncertainty and Profit
		Macro	Schumpeter's Theory of Economic Development

Source Own elaboration

2.2   Identity Theory for n-Culturals

This approach helps to understand and explain certain social phenomena in the face of the diverse indigenous cultures that existed before colonization throughout Latin America, mainly by the Spanish and Portuguese. This cultural heterogeneity of indigenous peoples is often incompatible with the basic assumptions of mainstream theories. It requires drawing on different sets of cultural values to understand the phenomenon.

Other theoretical approaches have covered the topic from the study of indigenous entrepreneurship, which is among the youngest fields of academic research, revealing that some cultural values cannot be studied with existing mainstream theories of entrepreneurship (Dana, 2007).

In this context, Latin America is a rich region to explore and study this phenomenon. With more than 54 million people of indigenous origin, which corresponds to 8.5% of the total population (Fierro, 2020; Psacharopoulos & Patrinos, 1994), the understanding and study of indigenous cultural heterogeneity could shed light on the current social phenomena and the heterogeneity of family businesses in the region. Especially since indigenous culture is heterogeneous in geographical distribution and in the degrees of syncretization, which is how the symbiosis of two cultures, European and indigenous, developed.

The organization among indigenous peoples is often based on kinship ties, which were not necessarily created in response to market needs. In contrast to Western-style capitalism, some indigenous economies show egalitarianism, collectivity, and community activity (Peredo et al., 2004). From these elements, indigenous entrepreneurship is often based on available resources, and working in communities may be less regular than in traditional societies. As a result, much of the entrepreneurial activity among indigenous peoples involves non-transactional economic activity.

Identity Theory for n-Culturals posits that there are individuals who operate at the intersection of multiple cultures while maintaining the salience of their cultural identities (Pekerti, 2019). This approach illustrates that n-culturals are active in their organizations because they are creative synthesizers who can facilitate organizational goals and serve as role models for others who are developing in a multicultural environment.

One of the elements of this principle is individual identity composed of personal identity, e.g., physical attributes, psychological traits, skills and interests, and social identity related to group dynamics and classifications. Under this framework, the study of syncretism defines this cultural exchange that took place for more than 200 years (Pekerti & Thomas, 2016).

2.3   Lee's Theory

Migration is broadly defined as a change of permanent or semi-permanent residence. No restrictions are placed on the distance of movement or the voluntary or involuntary nature of the act, and no distinction is made between external and internal migration. The decision to migrate is not rational, and for some people, the rational component is much less than the irrational. This model also explains that the volume of migration within a given territory varies with the degree of diversity in it. If migration results from a favorable consideration of origin and destination, a high degree of diversity between areas should lead to high levels of migration. Under such conditions, opportunities arise that are sufficient to attract people whose dissatisfaction with their places of origin is little more than the minimum, as reflected in the case of different migration flows (Goldstein, 1958).

Lee's (1966) migration model describes the push and pull factors of migration. A push factor is something unfavorable about a region in which someone experiences and thus is a reason for them to leave. A pull factor attracts someone to an area. It can be economic, cultural, or environmental. This model does not isolate particular push and pull factors; every place has several positive, negative, and neutral attributes.

Some examples of push factors could be war, famine, drought, and lack of jobs. Examples of pull factors are better living conditions such as work opportunities. Under this framework, migration is selective due to differences in personal factors, conditions in origin and destination, and intervening obstacles that are handled differently among individuals. Selectivity can be both positive and negative. It is positive when there is a high-quality selection of migrants and negative when selecting low quality. Migrants who respond to positive factors at destination tend to be positively selected; conversely, migrants who respond to negative factors at origin tend to be negatively selected.

As in all different migration flows in Latin America, the greatest tendency to migrate took place at certain stages of the colonization and independence cycle. The heterogeneity of the migrants also had a high correlation between the population characteristics in the place of origin and the place of destination.

2.4   Internal Social Capital

Family business scholars have theorized from the perspective of social capital since it offers a unique position to address the family business features and understand their collective actions and the outcomes associated with the groups' inter-individual interplay.

One way of using this theory is through the distinct set of resources embedded in relationships (Borgatti et al., 1998). Taking this perspective, the analysis focuses on external linkages and the benefits that arise from structural gaps found within the network of relationships. Thus, social capital is derived from an external focus on direct or indirect ties between those inside the collective network and outside it.

On the other hand, Hoffman et al. (2006) conceptualize social capital as a way to identify the existing resources within people's relationships. For example, social trust, norms, and networks allow the cooperation and coordination of participants for mutual benefit and to act more effectively when pursuing common goals (Putnam, 2001).

From the micro point of view, social capital involves the creation of entities composed of social structures that enable actions among actors, i.e., corporate actors or individuals, within a structure. As a resource, social capital is a consequence of the relationships between communities, individuals, societies, or organizations (Bolino et al., 2002) and it is represented by three key elements: structural, opportunity, and action-oriented (Lin, 1999). We use the Internal Social Capital model of Nahapiet and Ghoshal (1998), in which they present a conceptualizing framework of social capital in the development of intellectual capital.

2.5   Resource-Based View

The resource-based view applies to family firms that are already able to develop unique competitive advantages given the various resources that arise from family involvement, with certain intangibles such as patient capital and human capital (Habbershon & Williams, 1999). This framework contributes to knowledge the behavior of entrepreneurs when they are embedded in a larger social network structure that constitutes a significant proportion of their opportunity structure. According to Eckhardt and Shane (2003), people individually can discern whether an entrepreneurial opportunity exists but may lack the social connections to turn the opportunity into a new venture. The same study indicates that access to a more extensive social network could help overcome this lack of resources to seize opportunities.

In a Latin American context of large family economic groups, this framework helps us understand the use of their dynamic capabilities and how these firms have been able to outperform their competitors by using their resources and capabilities, which are unique to the firm and unmatched by competitors. These include all the assets, capabilities, organizational processes, firm attributes, information, knowledge, and professional and family norms that have enabled the development of a strategy for growth and adaptation in a fast-changing environment.

We have mainly focused on the development stage of these major economic groups: on those assets that have been a source of above-normal returns, the intangible organizational resources, the development of networks in governments, and partnerships with other companies. These intangible assets seem to be difficult to imitate or replace by other types of organizations, given that they are asymmetrically distributed in the various industries where family businesses in the region have developed, both in the manufacturing and service sectors.

2.6   Theory of Institutional Change

The theory of institutional change provides us with a conceptual framework to examine the interactions between organizations and the institutional environment within the concept of institutional quality (DiMaggio & Powell, 1983). It is especially interesting to apply this framework in Latin America given the stability (or instability) of the rules of the game historically, which are fundamental in shaping a society (North, 1990). Under this theory, the use of the institutional context consists of how regulatory, normative, and cultural arrangements interact to stimulate or limit the economic and social activities that family economic groups have developed during this period. Likewise, institutional change includes the existence of formal institutions, explicit rules, controls, and rewards as well as other prescriptive, evaluative, and obligatory dimensions in social life (Granovetter, 1985).

Particularly the family business in Latin America and specifically the development of economic groups has required that they must interpret legal expectations and non-formal cues for business development and expansion. In fact, the institutional environment can define and limit the prevailing norms and affect the structure of market players, including the size of existing organizations and the type of new emerging firms (Aldrich & Cliff, 2003). Furthermore, institutional theorists stress that, due to the set of constraints in the external institutional context, organizational behaviors tend to become isomorphic over time (Aldrich & Ruef, 2006; Zucker, 1977). This means that firms can easily imitate and substitute themselves as individual market players, and therefore, cannot establish ex-post and ex-ante boundaries that strengthen the sustainability of their competitive advantages.

This behavior is very evident in the growth processes of large family groups in Latin America; as these companies internationalize, family managers are expected to play an increasingly important role in managing their foreign expansion. As a specific resource, family managers are closely adjusted to the institutional environment of the host country. Therefore, they must carefully decide where family managers should be assigned, as there may be positions within the business groups that are more crucial than others.

2.7   The Theory of Uncertainty and Profit

The entrepreneurial function involves the discovery, organization, and exploitation of opportunities, that is, making available to people new products, services, or production processes, new strategies and organizational forms, and new markets for products and inputs that did not exist before (Shane & Venkataraman, 2000). This action has risks, more than just economic risks, but also involves environmental, political, and legal risks, among others. In this context, the entrepreneur—at the micro-level—uses intuition, stays alert, explores new businesses, starts new ways of acting, and identifies commercial opportunities.

With this theoretical framework used at the individual level, we want to explain the incentives and risks those global entrepreneurs in Latin America have had in the development of new businesses that have resulted in ventures that have crossed borders. In fact, new opportunities rarely arise rationally and predictably, but rather in the context of high uncertainty and long-term horizons (Bird & West, 1998), as is the Latin American scenario.

The point of Knight's (1921) theory of uncertainty and profit is that entrepreneurs are a group of people who take risks and deal with uncertainty. Knight further identifies the entrepreneur as the recipient of profit and points out that this profit is the entrepreneur's reward for bearing the costs of uncertainty. Risk is a situation in which the probabilities associated with a range of scenarios can be calculated, while uncertainty is a situation in which neither its probability distribution nor its mode of occurrence is known (Brockhaus, 1980). Keynes (1936), on the other hand, focused on describing that risk has a reward on the forecasting and assessment of investment returns. The differentiation between risk and uncertainty has been somewhat overlooked by the neoclassical literature (Hodgson, 2011), and it may be critical in understanding the variability of returns when the entrepreneur is in a high uncertainty environment.

2.8 Schumpeter's Theory of Economic Development

Schumpeter's particular concept of the entrepreneur applies to the model of global entrepreneurs presented in this text. The creation of new companies as a factor of economic development depends, according to Schumpeter, on the behavior of the entrepreneur who carries out a new combination of productive factors. As we shall see in the corresponding section, the new global entrepreneurs in Latin America, despite the in many cases adverse circumstances for entrepreneurship, carry out an innovative process, a new production function.

Opportunities for new combinations of factors of production stem mainly from observing the environment, managing technological change, and proximity to end-users. For Schumpeter, an entrepreneur is anyone who "carves out new combinations of the factors of production" and, therefore, includes not only the "... independent businessmen in an exchange economy who are usually so designated, but all who actually fulfill the function by which we define the concept, even if they are dependent, employees of a company, like managers, members of boards of directors, and so forth" (Schumpeter, 1912: 74–75). They cease to be entrepreneurs as soon as they set up their company and begin to manage the business on a day-to-day basis. To illustrate Schumpeter's theory in this text, Latin American entrepreneurs are distinctive by both type and behavior, and in the cases presented, we can differentiate entrepreneurs from owners-managers of small firms and entrepreneurial firms from small firms.

The theoretical approaches used in this text are not intended to be exhaustive; rather, they are meant to demonstrate to the family business, entrepreneurship scholars, and practitioners in this field to concisely outline the many different pathways available for theoretical and empirical exploration of the complexity of the study of heterogeneity in Latin American family business. Too often, family business research is consigned to a simplistic, binomial perspective of family and non-family business research when the research opportunities abound if we change the nature of our research questions and time scale. Therefore, following Payne (2018), we have conceived this text from a descriptive and comparative question to how and why, which are explanatory and predictive questions. However, in the light of this text, it is necessary to further develop new theories, new constructs, and a new timeline by borrowing theoretical frameworks from other fields that have applicability to the region's reality and dynamics. Family business researchers in Latin America should incorporate the specificities of the Latin American context in their research, and the best way to achieve this is to reinterpret the role of Latin American families in business in their research.

Historical patterns in Latin America make this geographic region a testing ground to advance research on the diversity of family structure and composition based on family geographic location, family religion, family country of origin, migration flows, and family culture, all of which could reveal essential specificities of business families.

References

Aldrich, H. E., & Cliff, J. E. (2003). The pervasive effects of family on entrepreneurship: Toward a family embeddedness perspective. *Journal of Business Venturing, 18*(5), 573–596.

Aldrich, H. E., & Ruef, M. (2006). *Organizations evolving*. SAGE Publications Ltd. https://www.doi.org/10.4135/9781446212509.

Bird, B. J., & West, G. P., III. (1998). Time and entrepreneurship. *Entrepreneurship Theory and Practice, 22*(2), 5–9.

Bolino, M. C., Turnley, W. H., & Bloodgood, J. M. (2002). Citizenship behavior and the creation of social capital in organizations. *Academy of Management Review, 27*(4), 505–522.

Borgatti, S. P., Jones, C., & Everett, M. G. (1998). Network measures of social capital. *Connections, 21*(2), 27–36.

Botero, I. C., Discua Cruz, A., & Müller, C. G. (2019). Family firms in Latin America: Why are they important and why should we care? In C. G. Müller, I. C. Botero, A. Discua Cruz, & R. Subramanian (Eds.), *Family firms in Latin America* (pp. 1–8). Routledge.

Brockhaus, R. H., Sr. (1980). Risk taking propensity of entrepreneurs. *Academy of Management Journal, 23*(3), 509–520.

Clinton, R. N. (1989). A brief history of the adoption of the United States constitution. *Iowa Law Review, 75*, 891.

Dana, L. P. (2007). *International handbook of research on indigenous entrepreneurship*. Edward Elgar Publishing.

DiMaggio, P. J., & Powell, W. W. (1983). The iron cage revisited: Institutional isomorphism and collective rationality in organizational fields. *American Sociological Review*, 147–160.

Donnelley, R. G. (1964). The family business. *Harvard Business Review, 42*(4), 93–105.

Eckhardt, J. T., & Shane, S. A. (2003). Opportunities and entrepreneurship. *Journal of Management, 29*(3), 333–349.

Fierro, J. (2020). Indigenous people, redistribution, and support for the political regime in Latin America. *Acta Politica*, 1–21.

Goldstein, S. (1958). *Patterns of mobility, 1910–1950*.

Gomez-Mejia, L., Basco, R., Gonzalez, A. C., & Muller, C. G. (2020). Family business and local development in Iberoamerica. *Cross Cultural and Strategic Management*.

Gomez-Mejia, L. R., Cruz, C., Berrone, P., & De Castro, J. (2011). The bind that ties: Socioemotional wealth preservation in family firms. *Academy of Management Annals, 5*(1), 653–707.

Granovetter, M. (1985). Economic action and social structure: The problem of embeddedness. *American Journal of Sociology, 91*(3), 4.

Guajardo-Trevino, S. S. (2021). An exploratory study of the effects of socioemotional wealth in the perception of humanistic management and psychological ownership in family and non-family members in Latin American family firms. In *Humanistic management in Latin America* (pp. 111–133). Routledge.

Habbershon, T. G., & Williams, M. L. (1999). A resource-based framework for assessing the strategic advantages of family firms. *Family Business Review, 12*(1), 1–25.

Hodgson, G. M. (2011). The eclipse of the uncertainty concept in mainstream economics. *Journal of Economic Issues, 45*(1), 159–176.

Hoffman, J., Hoelscher, M., & Sorenson, R. (2006). Achieving sustained competitive advantage: A family capital theory. *Family Business Review, 19*(2), 135–145.

Knight, F. (1921). *Risk, uncertainty and profit*. Augustus Kelley.

Keynes, J. M. (1936). The supply of gold. *The Economic Journal, 46*(183), 412–418.

Lee, E. (1966). A theory of migration. *Demography, 3*(1), 47–57. https://doi.org/10.2307/2060063.

Lin, N. (1999). Social networks and status attainment. *Annual Review of Sociology, 25*(1), 467–487.

Marjański, A., & Sułkowski, Ł. (2020). Entrepreneurial family businesses in Poland: From an emerging to a developed market. In *Entrepreneurial finance in emerging markets* (pp. 87–101). Palgrave Macmillan.

Melin, L., Nordqvist, M., & Sharma, P. (Eds.). (2014). *The SAGE handbook of family business*. Sage.

Memili, E., & Dibrell, C. (Eds.). (2019). *The Palgrave handbook of heterogeneity among family firms*. Cham: Palgrave Macmillan.

Miller, D., & Le Breton-Miller, I. (2021). Family firms: A breed of extremes? *Entrepreneurship Theory and Practice, 45*(4), 663–681. https://doi.org/10.1177/1042258720964186.

Nahapiet, J., & Ghoshal, S. (1998). Social capital, intellectual capital, and the organizational advantage. *Academy of Management Review, 23*(2), 242–266.

North, D. (1990). An introduction to institutions and institutional change. *Institutions, Institutional Change and Economic Performance, 3*–10.

Parada, M. J., Müller, C., & Gimeno, A. (2016). Family firms in Ibero-America: an introduction. *Academia Revista Latinoamericana de Administración*.

Payne, G. T. (2018). *Reflections on family business research: Considering domains and theory*.

Pekerti, A. A. (2019). Identity theory for n-Culturals. In *n-culturalism in managing work and life* (pp. 9–19). Springer, Cham.

Pekerti, A. A., & Thomas, D. C. (2016). n-Culturals: Modeling the multicultural identity. *Cross Cultural and Strategic Management*.

Peredo, A. M., Anderson, R. B., Galbraith, C. S., Honig, B., & Dana, L. P. (2004). Towards a theory of indigenous entrepreneurship. *International Journal of Entrepreneurship and Small Business, 1*(1–2), 1–20.

Psacharopoulos, G., & Patrinos, H. A. (Eds.). (1994). *Indigenous people and poverty in Latin America: An empirical analysis*. The World Bank.

Putnam, R. (2001). Social capital: Measurement and consequences. *Canadian Journal of Policy Research, 2*(1), 41–51.

Schumpeter, J. A. (1912). Theorie der Wirtschaftlichen Entwicklung [English translation, 1934: *The Theory of Economic Development*. Harvard University Press]. Duncker and Humblot.

Shane, S., & Venkataraman, S. (2000). The promise of entrepreneurship as a field of research. *Academy of Management Review, 25*(1), 217–226.

Stangej, O., & Basco, R. (2017). The entrepreneurial role of families in transitional economies: The case of Lithuania. In *Entrepreneurship in transition economies* (pp. 345–365). Springer, Cham.

Worthman, M. S. (1994). Theoretical foundations for family-owned business: A conceptual research-based paradigm. *Family Business Review, 7*, 3–27.

Zucker, L. G. (1977). The role of institutionalization in cultural persistence. *American Sociological Review*, 726–743.

3

The Syncretism (The First Wave): The First Family Business in the Region

In this chapter, we will reflect on Latin American family businesses, which are, in the first instance, the result of the roots of what makes up the meaning of the "Latinoamericano," based on the syncretism (mixture) of different cultures, mainly from the Spanish one, with the native indigenous groups. This characteristic makes family businesses heterogeneous from the outset. Illustratively, this section shows two paradigmatic cases of family businesses that converged on this syncretism: Jose Cuervo Tequila/Mexico Founded: 1758 and Hacienda Los Lingues Ranch/Chile Founded: 1760, which are the oldest family firms in Latin America.

It is also important to mention that the roots of family businesses in Latin America have to do with the context of the pre-Columbian and colonial economy in which they emerged and which allowed them to leave a cultural heritage that is preserved to this day.

Therefore, this chapter provides the reader with the following Learning objectives:

© The Author(s), under exclusive license to Springer Nature
Switzerland AG 2021
C. G. Müller and F. Sandoval-Arzaga, *Family Business Heterogeneity in Latin America*, Palgrave Studies in Family Business Heterogeneity,
https://doi.org/10.1007/978-3-030-78931-2_3

- To understand the historical process of Latin American syncretism as the basis for the appearance of the first family businesses in the continent.
- To analyze two successful cases of continuity of Latin American family businesses that survive until today and that are the product of this period.

3.1   The Notion of the Latin American Concept

Several authors have debated the "Latin American" concept at different times. It was first used at a conference in Paris in 1856 given by the Chilean politician Francisco Bilbao Barquín, who included not only South America but also Mexico and Central America.[1] Today the Pan-Hispanic Dictionary of Doubts of the Royal Spanish Academy defines Latin America as the name that encompasses all the countries of the American continent in which Latin-derived languages (Spanish, Portuguese and French) are spoken, as opposed to English-speaking America.

These regions, within America, do not always or necessarily correspond to national borders. Hence, the concept of Latin America can also be grasped in a cultural sense in which a unitary identity is sought, and it is this uniformity that is questioned faced with the plurality of societies that make up Latin America. That is why the author Alain Rouquié (1989) prefers to call it "Latin Americas." The truth is that, as this author mentions, a more concrete way to define it is as the part of America conquered by the Spanish and Portuguese.

The European colonization of America was a painful process that was plagued by numerous conquerors abuses against the native peoples, including wars, massacres, sexual abuse, slavery, and pandemics, in which

---

[1] "Latin or South America?". *Clarín*, 16 May 2005. https://www.clarin.com/ediciones-anteri ores/america-latina-sudamerica_0_BkHMQbYJCYl.html.

it is estimated that 90% of the indigenous population (approximately 54 million people[2]) disappeared.

At the same time, there was a syncretic process in which the pre-Columbian peoples adopted the Christian religion mixed with the indigenous one. As Octavio Paz wrote: "Syncretism appeared [...]: the Indians converted to Christianity and, simultaneously, converted angels and saints into pre-Hispanic gods" (12).[3] The most privileged example, Jacques Lafaye tells us, of this syncretism between ancient America and Christianity is Quetzalcoatl-Saint Thomas "in which two worlds advanced towards each other" (280).[4] In other words, it is a space in which the colonized is identified with the colonizer.

The concrete form of syncretism was reflected in racial and cultural miscegenation. The mixing of ethnic groups occurred between three racial groups: the white (European), the Indigenous (pre-Hispanic), and the black (brought from Africa). This resulted in 16 different combinations and determined both caste system and class domination. The mestizo (son of Spanish or Portuguese and Indigenous) was rejected by Europeans and Indigenouss because he was in the middle of the social system: he had more privileges than the Indigenous but less than the Europeans.

This class system was justified from the perspective that "civilization" was what the Spanish and Portuguese brought to the New World; that is, it had to be imposed from the "metropolis" to the "colony." Thus a dichotomous way of life was established in which it was necessary to imitate the Europeans, be like them, and at the same time it was necessary to reject them in order to free oneself from European domination. It is in this scenario that a part of the Creoles (sons of Spaniards or Portuguese born in America) took a position more in favor of the Indigenouss than the Europeans, at the same time seeking to break the bond

---

[2] Koch, A., Brierley, C., Maslin, M. M., & Lewis, S. L. (2019). Earth system impacts of the European arrival and Great Dying in the Americas after 1492. *Quaternary Science Reviews, 207*, 13–36.

[3] Preface of: Lafaye, J. (2015). *Quetzalcóatl y Guadalupe: La formación de la conciencia nacional en México: Abismo de conceptos: Identidad, nación, mexicano.* Fondo de cultura económica.

[4] Lafaye, J. (2015). *Quetzalcóatl y Guadalupe: La formación de la conciencia nacional en México: Abismo de conceptos: Identidad, nación, mexicano.* Fondo de cultura económica.

that united them to the metropolis and become the new oligarchic class, which gave rise to modernity. As Bolívar Echeverría tells us: "Modernity itself is a multiple event that thus affects, with its own multiplicity, the multiplicity that comes from the past".[5]

European and the pre-Columbian civilizations, and the African and Asian; it is a mixture in which it was not possible to annihilate or totally impose one worldview over another: it is a mixture full of contradictions, of acceptance, imitation, rejection, and liberation. And it is in this context in which economic activities that had a relevant impact on colonial life were incorporated, from which the first Latin American family businesses emerged, businesses that from their roots, as we can see from now on, will be heterogeneous by nature, made up with elements of different class and nature.

3.2 The Origin of the Latin American Economy

3.2.1 Pre-Columbian Economy

To understand the emergence of the first family businesses in Latin America, we must understand what the economy was like before and during the colonial era. The pre-Columbian economy was varied given the vast region it encompassed, as well as its types of climate, ecosystems, and the differences in the pre-Hispanic cultures. Thus, the economy ranged from hunting and gathering plants to more advanced agricultural systems and specialized economies, such as ceramics and jewelry.

In many autonomous indigenous villages, the economy consisted of a domestic mode of production where self-sufficiency was the basis; each family had its own land, animals, and plants to cover its food needs. Families were in charge of making clothes, utensils, and tools while collecting water for heating and cooking. They produced their own

---

[5] In "La clave barroca en América Latina". Bolívar Echeverría. Exposition at the Latein-Amerika Institut of the Freie Universität Berlin, November 2002. Published on the website "Bolívar Echeverría. Critical discourse and philosophy of culture".

pottery and used stones and minerals to make their tools and utensils. Men and women had different tasks in this system: men hunted, fished, and made their stone tools while women cooked, stored water and made pottery, with agriculture as a shared task (Storey & Widmer, 2006). This domestic form of family-based production could be considered as one of the first antecedents or roots of the first "family businesses" and could resemble a today's type of family business called Family Team (Gimeno et al., 2010) in which the mental model by which they act is one in which the family has a high dedication to the business and works together for it. Examples of this type of family business could be the fondas or family restaurants where the whole family participates, they are not interested in growing and it is only a means of subsistence for the family.

A fundamental element in the pre-Columbian economy was the lack of domesticated animals used as transportation vehicles, which limited the development of the agricultural economy, since human labor was the main source of energy. The only exception was the llama, but it was only used for light loads and at high altitudes in Peru (Inca culture). On the other hand, this characteristic may have allowed pre-Columbian peoples to develop sophisticated engineering systems of transportation to carry water, promote long-distance trade and develop irrigation systems that competed with those of the Old World (Slicher, 1992; Storey & Widmer, 2006). Notable examples of these irrigation engineering developments and agricultural production methods of the Mesoamerican and Central American plateau are the milpa as a system of ridges and furrows in the field, or the chinanmpas, floating planting fields in water channels that also served as a transportation system; in South America, the complex of cordilleras, water channels for cultivation in large extensions; or the camellones in the Andes where salinization was mitigated, or qocha agriculture in the Titikaka basin. The improvement of agriculture and an increase in population were consequences of these hydraulic works. This is a period in which "full-time labor specialization, social stratification and the construction of urbanized ceremonial centers" (Escalante P., 2004: 162) originated. It will also be the basis of a regional diversity of peoples in Mesoamerica with different architectural styles, religious, and artistic rites, which was strengthening a regional maturity that allowed the consolidation of a noble class that exercised command functions to wage wars, manage the market, and organize cities. This diversity of regional peoples and the consolidation of two empires was what the Spanish and Portuguese faced before the conquest.

Before the arrival of the Spanish and Portuguese in Brazil, the indigenous peoples were widely dispersed, with the Guarani and Tupi cultures being two of the most relevant. In the Mesoamerican plateau, Central America and South America in general, the main cultures were the Maya and Teotihuacan first, and the Aztec and Inca later. Both developed large urban centers and cities. It is therefore not surprising that the development of the pre-Columbian economy took place in these dominant peoples with more consolidated political, social, and hierarchical poles. The Mexican and Andean societies were based on agriculture, in high-altitude areas with imperial organizations (Noejovich, 1996).

For example, Teotihuacan was the first urban development in central Mexico and one of the largest pre-industrial cities in the Old World. It was in the villages or hamlets around the great city where the economic activities of agriculture, cattle raising, and fishing took place. In Teotihuacan there were several socioeconomic activities without great distinctions of social classes, but organized in multifamily complexes with a clearly hierarchical structure. It is estimated that 20 families lived in each complex, which were usually dedicated to the same trade and were relatives; it was a patrilocal system since it was discovered that the ties between men were closer than that of women, i.e., the latter went to live in the complexes with the men (Escalante P., 2004). Escalante (2004) states that there were four essential characteristics in these multifamily complexes: (1) they were corporate groups in the form of clans that made up the neighborhood, (2) some families were richer than others, which made a differentiation between the corporate groups, (3) the neighborhoods of artisans, farmers, and other workers had urban infrastructure with streets, drainage, solid housing, which means that it was not a poor class, and (4) there were buildings of a wide decoration that were the homes of the nobles. That is, Teotihuacan was a clear corporate structure that made it grow in a sustained manner (Manzanilla Naim, 2018). When the work was extended, usually agricultural, and exceeded the primary family nucleus, uncles, cousins, and aunts who lived in the same community were incorporated (multifamily) and constituted socioeconomic units through lineage (Storey & Widmer, 2006). This multifamily idea with diverse economic activities and a corporate hierarchical structure can form a current antecedent of the so-called Family Business Groups, where a family or several families control or manage a group of companies or businesses (Rautiainen et al., 2019) and in which they need a corporate family and business structure to sustain themselves.

Other essential characteristics of the pre-Columbian economy, in addition to household production, were redistribution and reciprocal exchange (Storey & Widmer, 2006). Redistribution consisted of the surplus produced by families being given to elites (political, religious and military) for their consumption. And in some populations this surplus was returned to the families that had given it in times of scarcity, which constituted a kind of insurance.

On the other hand, reciprocal exchange consisted of giving products in exchange for others, sometimes with similar characteristics or functions and sometimes not (for example, jewelry for clothing), which helped to cover diverse needs. But it also fulfilled diverse functions; for example, alliances were formed between families and groups, it served as a socio-political element when the chiefs of the elites between different peoples exchanged valuable materials for each of them (minerals, skins, figurines, and artistic artifacts, feathers, etc.) as a sign of friendship or subordination. In some cases these exchanges also fulfilled sacred or religious functions. Therefore, it is not strange that when the Spaniards and Portuguese arrived, they received them with gifts.

Markets were thus generated and the dominant or imperial peoples of Mexico and the Andes, who controlled other smaller peoples and large tracts of land, collected tribute as part of their political and economic system to secure resources and raw materials .

This was, in general terms, the economy upon the arrival of the Europeans in the New World, and from there, new methods and forms of production were mixed to create the colonial economy.

3.2.2 Colonial Economy

After the Conquest, the colonial economy began to be created, with a diversification of economic activities, which led to the establishment of a market economy, although the subsistence economy of pre-Columbian times did not disappear. The economic activities were mainly farming and agriculture, livestock, hunting, fishing, trade, transportation, and mineral exploitation. Regarding the domestic market, livestock activities were developed, especially sheep and cattle breeding, as well as silkworm breeding; there was also wheat and sugar production and the exploitation of gold and silver mines. In the foreign market, trade was generated between Mexico, Peru, and Spain; and, at the same time, between Brazil and Portugal in the exchange of silver, dyes, and manufactured tools, textiles, and furniture. All of this led to new means of transportation and the use of currency as a means of payment, which generated the capitalist market economy system. Basically, the colonial economic system was based on the generation of production surpluses that could be sent to the metropolis. Therefore, it was necessary to produce more than what was necessary to cover the basic needs of the population, as well as those goods that had a market in Europe. In order to achieve this, a system of economic servility was created, called "la mitad" or "la encomienda," in which a group of indigenous people were "entrusted" ("encomendados") to a European lord, usually giving him land, to produce these goods in exchange for evangelization and food. This system worked in places where there was a larger population, such as Mexico and Peru. In areas of low population density, such as Brazil, slaves were brought from Africa to do this work.

During the first century of the Colony the subsistence economy was predominant, but from the second century (1640–1750) the market economy began to gain strength. There was a period of the so-called "economic depression," due to the difficulty of finding European markets that could buy the surpluses in an attractive way but that financed and supplied wealth to the metropolis and the crown. It is in this century that the dominant powers of the colony were consolidated, that is to say, the church, the merchants, and the landowners. It is worth mentioning that it is precisely from the merchants and landowners that the first family businesses in Latin America emerged.

The colonial economy was based on population density and the differences between the city and the countryside. It is in the cities where the epicenter of commerce, as well as some industrial activities and the cultivation of vegetables are maintained, while in the outskirts, in the countryside, with low population density, large-scale agriculture, livestock and fishing activities are generated in large extensions (haciendas), in addition to mining.

And it is precisely mining, especially the exploitation of gold and silver, which generated the sustenance of the Colony since it was the currency used in the world. The economic system of the Colony depended to a great extent on the international prices of the production that took place in the periphery, production in which forced labor and encomienda were used, and which generated great concentrations of wealth in very few hands. Some of the products coveted by the European markets, in addition to mining, were tobacco, cotton, corn, cacao, sugar, as well as pearls and exotic animals.

Trade in the colonial economy had its greatest boom when the cities ceased to be only the passage of exports of silver and gold, in the mid-eighteenth century, to also become consumers of the world market when the Spanish colony, and later the Portuguese, relaxed their laws and allowed an increase in free trade, being pressured especially by England. New traders emerged, mainly in the field of transport and finance, as goods had to be redistributed internally to different cities within the colony. The improvement of urban services also caused large landowners to move to the cities, which increased local trade due to their greater purchasing power.

The first family businesses in colonial times arose precisely from this merchant class that was organized through the crown by the consulates, the two most important being those of Lima and Mexico. The members of these consulates were originally peninsulars who arrived in the

New World and involved their families in the trade business, creating (through the marriage of their daughters) commercial networks with their husbands in different parts of the New World and inheriting the business to their descendants, who in many cases were already Creoles. Thus, the community of merchants was created by business families who—through kinship relations—increased their business and created relational capital in the political sphere as well. At the same time, they diversified their businesses and invested their economic capital in other economic activities, particularly in mining and agriculture.

Although many of the haciendas in colonial times belonged to the clergy, the lay farmers were the owners of the first family businesses in Latin America along with the merchants. The hacienda, which was part of the evolution of the encomienda, meant domination of the land, the labor force (indigenous or slave), and also local commerce. The haciendas then, in their final structure, were a form of property in which the agricultural enterprise was combined with a stable settlement of population, in which they went from slave labor in its initial origin in the colony to free labor, that is, free people, usually mestizos, who preferred to work in the haciendas rather than pay tribute; they were laborers or wage earners who resided in the hacienda lands since they were somehow protected by them.

The first hacienda owners were the Spanish and Portuguese conquistadors. Later, high-ranking officials also owned haciendas. There were also small landowners (white farmers or ex-military) but they usually had large debts and ended up selling their properties. Even so, a class of small landowners emerged, of free persons who were also known as "rancheros" who leased their land from the hacienda owners. Finally, as already mentioned, merchants acquired haciendas to diversify their capital. Preponderant figures in the haciendas were the latifundios, that is, when the extension of land obtained was very large. The large estates were the ones that produced the greatest production surpluses, which led to an important change in the colonial economy.

It is in this context of pre-Columbian and later colonial economy that the first Latin American family businesses emerged and, as we will analyze in the following chapter, they have left a unique and heterogeneous cultural heritage that has been maintained to this day.

3.3   The Cultural Heritage of the Oldest Family Business in Latin America

Family businesses, from a historical perspective, are cultural artifacts that occur over time and are framed in a specific context. In this section, the context occurs in the syncretism originated in Latin America when pre-Columbian indigenous cultures came into contact with Spanish and Portuguese cultures, but also incorporating African culture.

Cultural heritage is defined as "the set of valuable objects and qualities that have been passed down from previous generations" (The New Oxford American Dictionary). In a family business, the valuable objects and qualities are its resources, competencies, identity, knowledge, and prestige that are transmitted intergenerationally.[6] In this way, the fact that the family business itself, as a cultural artifact, is perpetuated through the generations is part of the cultural heritage of the society in which it is immersed.

A cultural heritage of this historical period is related to the current concept of indigenous entrepreneurship[7], that is, the fact of introducing into the current market products or services of indigenous communities that result in local economic development, environmental protection and the preservation of indigenous culture. In this chapter, we have shown how in pre-Columbian (indigenous) times there was a subsistence economy, with the nuclear and extended family being the basis of production. Indigenous entrepreneurship is a result of cultural and family inheritance. In practically all Latin American countries, if one goes to any indigenous or tourist town, it is highly probable to find "indigenous entrepreneurial families" offering their products and services. Their current businesses come from this entire cultural heritage. An example of this is the care of the environment through ecotourism or the traditional products produced by indigenous artisans or gastronomy and medicinal

---

[6] These are the elements that Colli, Andrea (2011) identifies as part of the cultural heritage of family businesses and that are transmitted from one generation to the next. In this chapter we will take these elements, in an exercise of reflecting on how they have endured or evolved for family businesses as a whole.

[7] To delve into this concept we suggest reading Peredo, A. M. et al. (2004) and Dana, L. P. (2015) who propose indigenous entrepreneurship as an emerging field of research.

herbs, among many others. Recent analyses of this cultural heritage are those carried out by Macpherson et al. (2021) on the Mapuche indigenous people in Chile and Molina-Ramírez and Barba-Sánchez (2021) on different indigenous peoples in Mexico.

Another cultural heritage of this era is linked to the also emerging concept of n-Culturals defined as the integration of different cultural identities simultaneously and that enriches individuals by giving them better capabilities to perform creatively, flexibly, and effectively interculturally (Pekerti & Thomas, 2016). What this theory refers to is precisely the syncretism that we described in the first section of this chapter. Current indigenous entrepreneurial families are n-Cultural by assimilating their own indigenous culture with the current Western business culture; an example of the above is the study by Tretiakov et al. (2020), which describes the Wayuu indigenous group of Colombia. We could venture to say that Latin American business families, and not only indigenous entrepreneurial families, are or have a great capacity to be n-Cultural because of the syncretism and multicultural mix in which the Latin American people have developed.

The concept of the family itself is one addition to the cultural legacy that has marked the identity and prestige of the Latin American family businesses. Particularly, the extended family, compared to the Anglo-Saxon culture, goes beyond the parent–offspring nucleus to include a larger family tree: grandparents, uncles, aunts, cousins, nephews, and even "compadres" (godfathers). The result is a blend of indigenous and European cultures that enabled the governance of Latin American family business by more informal, relational, and emotional mechanisms as opposed to other cultures that have more formal, cold, and rational mechanisms.

Another important contribution to the cultural heritage of colonial-era family businesses was their philanthropic work. Much of this contribution came from the Catholic Church providing education, food, and health care to the poorest as part of evangelization. These were pious works, called "Obras Pías." There also came to be individual Obras Pías, especially in the area of building hospitals and schools (Almaraz A., 2014). Even Hernán Cortés, the conqueror of New Spain, was an important philanthropist. Most of the individual philanthropists were the large landowners, hacendados, and merchants, who in turn were mainly family businesses that decided to support the poor and underprivileged, given the commitment they had already acquired in the region. Their donations were mainly in kind (usually real estate) or in cash, being the great part of these donations destined to the construction of hospitals and schools that were founded by the religious orders. The donation to the hospitals was given due to the various epidemics that the region suffered in different stages and that caused a very important decrease in the population.

An example of philanthropic activities was that of the family of Juan Nicolás Aguirre, a Chilean who bequeathed part of his patrimony to the construction of a hospice in the center of Santiago de Chile in 1758. Another type of philanthropic activity of family businessmen was the creation of the Monte de Piedad, that is, lending houses with a clear sense of social assistance. A model of this type of activity was that of the Mexican Pedro Romero de Terreros, known as the Count of Regla, who by 1775 was considered the richest man in America and possibly in the world, thanks to the exploitation of silver and gold mines, as well as haciendas. In 1775 he founded the Real Monte de Piedad in Mexico City, and contributed large sums of money in cash to convents and schools founded by religious.

The current economic structure of capitalism in Latin America is made up of large family economic groups in diversified sectors that form oligopolies and hierarchies. This structure has not changed much and is maintained as a cultural inheritance from the haciendas, large estates, and merchant communities of colonial times. The "institutional rigidity" or "path dependency" of this economic composition is part of a history that has not been able to change or evolve sufficiently.

In general, family businesses of the time have also left as a cultural heritage a contribution to the progress of Latin American countries and their peoples, by committing themselves to their region through philanthropic activities, in addition to providing an economic spillover to the groups of influence close to them and an increase in the dynamism of the market.

3.4 Case Studies

3.4.1 Grupo Cuervo

Grupo Cuervo is one of the longest family-owned companies in the American continent with a tradition of 11 generations. In 1758 it began its history with the title of Land Property, acquired by Don José Antonio de Cuervo y Valdés, whose main activity was the cultivation of agave. These lands were part of Nueva Galicia and were particularly concentrated in what is now Tequila (Jalisco, Mexico).

His son José María Guadalupe Cuervo y Montaño obtained the license in 1795 to produce Mezcal issued by Carlos IV. His brother José Prudencio acquired in 1781 some pastures of the "De Abajo" hacienda that would later become the Cuervo Tavern (Distillery). In 1805 the production of mezcals was already quite considerable and the town of Tequila became one of the richest in the Guadalajara area. Upon the death of José Guadalupe, he left his properties to José Ignacio Faustino and María Magdalena de Cuervo who married Vicente Albino Rojas and to whom he gave all his properties.

For this reason, in 1812 Vicente Albino Rojas changed the name of the Cuervo Distillery to La Rojeña, which is recognized as the oldest in Latin America. Don Vicente Rojas managed to considerably increase the assets ceded by his wife by distributing mezcal not only in Jalisco but also in other cities in Mexico. By the middle of the nineteenth century it was the most famous distillery in Tequila and already had more than three million agaves planted. Three owners were key to the growth of Grupo Cuervo in the nineteenth century: Don Vicente Rojas, Jesús Flores and José Cuervo Labastida.

Jesús Flores becomes the owner when the daughters of Don Vicente Rojas give him the rights to La Rojeña. Jesús Flores manages to promote the distillery again, maintaining it as one of the most important in the region. This was due to the arrival of the train that allowed distribution to more regions of Mexico and possibly to the United States. He also modernized the production process by making technological innovations. In 1880 in the city of Guadalajara they had already sold 10 thousand barrels (approximately 660 thousand liters). Part of the innovations of Don Jesús Flores was to bottle Tequila in glass containers, because before it was only sold in barrels. Jesús Flores marries for the second time, to Ana González Rubio.

In 1900, after the death of Don Jesús Flores at the age of 72, Ana González Rubio married José Cuervo Labastida and that is when the famous José Cuervo Tequila was born. Jose Cuervo was a descendant of the founders and received the patents and trademarks that endorsed Jose Cuervo Tequila, the industrial brands "Cuervo" and "La Rojeña." In the first decade of 1900, Jose Cuervo won highly recognized international awards in Madrid and Paris. Jose Cuervo and his wife Ana Gonzalez were very much loved in the community of Tequila thanks to the donations and support they gave to the church and the town (such as supplying it with water or the construction of a hospital). In 1910, with the beginning of the Mexican Revolution, of the 87 distilleries that Cuervo had, only 32 remained. In 1921 Jose Cuervo died, leaving Ana Gonzalez at the helm once again. During these years the production of Tequila was not the best, besides suffering affectations to its properties with the decree of the President of Mexico (Lázaro Cárdenas) of the distribution of the lands.

Guadalupe Gallardo, Ana González's niece, inherits the assets. The company managed to resist thanks to the administration of Guillermo Freytag Schreir until the reactivation of the market with the arrival of World War II. In 1957, Guadalupe and Guillermo's son, Guillermo Freytag Gallardo, manages the company until 1964. It was during this period that the famous Margarita Cocktail was created. Later, Guadalupe's grandnephew, Juan Beckmann Gallardo (son of Virginia Gallardo and Juan Beckmann, German consul in the city of Guadalajara) manages the company maintaining the industrial impulse like his predecessors. Upon the death of Virginia Gallardo, she left her four sons (Juan, Jorge, Carlos, and Oskar) the inheritance of the company and the properties.

In 1972 Juan Francisco Beckmann Vidal took over the management of Grupo Cuervo, giving it an important expansion both domestically and internationally. In 1974 they succeeded in promoting Tequila as a denomination of origin. Currently, Don Juan Francisco Beckmann Vidal is still Chairman of the Board of Directors and his son Juan Domingo Beckmann Legorreta is the Chief Executive Officer. Today the company produces, markets, and distributes in more than 85 countries with a portfolio of more than 30 brands of different alcoholic and non-alcoholic beverages.

3.4.2 Hacienda Los Lingues

Hacienda Los Lingues dates back to 1575, in the central valley of Chile, when it was a wine cellar, and today it is undoubtedly the oldest family business in the continent with 19 generations. It was founded by Melchor Jufré del Águila, who was a chronicler and writer of his city as well as mayor of the capital in 1599. When he died, the inheritance corresponded to Ana María Águila, wife of the governor of Chile, Diego González Montero, and from then on it has been passed on to 17 generations uninterruptedly. Both are ancestors of the Chilean Independence hero, Don José Gregorio Argomedo y Montero del Águila. The current owner of Los Lingues is Mr. Germán Claro Lira.

Los Lingues have a fine horse breeding farm founded in 1760 and considered one of the best in America. Its origins date back to the horses of the Berbers and Numidians in North Africa, brought to Spain by the Moors, and finally brought to the "New World" by the Spanish conquistadors.

For centuries Los Lingues developed activities typical of the haciendas of their time, mainly agriculture and wine, producing their own food and providing services to their owners, their workers, and their families. Even today many of the workers and families live in the facilities provided by the family.

In 1965, Germán Claro Lira began the process of seeking additional markets and restoring the main hacienda. This is how the boutique hotel was created and became one of the most important tourist destinations in the region, being the first Chilean country house that could be visited. He also created a real estate company that allowed him to develop projects in different parts of the country. However, he continues to maintain the horse breeding and wine business. This family, in its current generations, is a clear example of what it means to be an enterprising family in the search to remain in force for many more generations.

3.5   Conclusions

In this chapter we have reflected on how the Latin American concept is a product of syncretism, of the mixture of cultures between the indigenous world and the Latin-speaking Europeans. Before the arrival of the Spanish and Portuguese, indigenous peoples were already diverse in their cultural, religious, and economic practices. Throughout Latin America there were different regional peoples who managed to consolidate a noble class that took command and formed different alliances and dominant empires. Upon the arrival of the conquistadors in the New World, this miscegenation implied the introduction of new economic activities that were maintained alongside the previous ones, which had effects both within and outside the peoples. If society was already diverse with the encounter of the two worlds, it became even more so in all other areas: social, cultural, and economic. Thus, we have observed that Latin American family businesses are necessarily heterogeneous in their origin.

The emergence of the oldest family businesses in Latin America is understandable thanks to the pre-Columbian and colonial economies described in this chapter. In both economies it is the family (nuclear and extended, as well as its relationships) through which the production of goods and services emerges. Both in the role of the landowners and in that of the merchants, it is from where the first family businesses emerge, thanks also to the encomienda of the crown in the New World. In the pre-Columbian economy we observe two of the ways in which the Latin American family business was created. One is the subsistence economy and the other is the corporate structure of the big cities. In the subsistence economy it is the family nucleus that produces its own goods for self-consumption and we compare it with a current type of family business called Family Team (Gimeno et al., 2010) in which a family works together in the service of the family business. They are usually complex families, with a large number of family members owning and operating a small business. A Family Team is not interested in growing the family business but in maintaining it as part of the family subsistence. In the corporate structure, where a family clan is specialized in the production of goods not only for their subsistence but also in the surplus for the population and the nobility, which allows them to have benefits and a better standard of living, we made the comparison with what today can be called Family Business Groups, which bring together a set of companies with a corporate structure, which generate greater added value and have a set of privileges and power in the social hierarchical structure. In the colonial economy, although the previous form of production and trade was combined, new forms of trade and agricultural production arose, whose objective was both the exploitation of the indigenes and the exploitation of natural resources to send them to the crown. Thus arose the first family businesses on the continent, one of which was based on the encomienda, usually given to the conquistadors, and from which the haciendas controlled by a family nucleus were created and which we exemplify with two cases in this chapter. On the other hand, the market economy emerged with the export of resources and goods produced to the Old World, through settlers from Spain and Portugal, who formed family businesses, usually with relatives on both continents, who were in charge of these transactions.

The cultural heritage of the oldest family businesses can be seen clarified in concepts that emerge today, such as indigenous entrepreneurship or n-Culturals or also with the presence of large family groups that maintain the hierarchical and oligopolistic structures of the colonial era. The indigenous entrepreneurship in which goods and services of the native populations of Latin America are marketed has a clearly family base, since it is the artisans, farmers, or tourist servants grouped in families who offer these services, which have the objective of inserting these populations in the current economy and improving their standard of living, taking care of the traditions, customs, and ecosystems of these populations. The n-Culturals are based on the premise that economic and social performance is better if there is a mix of different cultures in an organization, that is to say, that diversity provokes a complementarity that adds value. Undoubtedly, the Latin American family business from its origins fulfills this condition since it is in essence, as we have already said, syncretic due to the mixture of its cultures.

The presence of family groups (landowners and transatlantic traders) that emerged in the pre-Columbian economy and consolidated in the colonial period, which we have called "the syncretic wave," had an important impact on the regional economic progress of Latin America, benefiting above all the metropolis, the privileged groups of the time and small groups of local artisan traders. Unfortunately, there was no benefit for the bulk of the population. This wealthy class also generated a rootedness in their region and developed philanthropic activities mainly oriented toward the construction of hospitals, schools, and confraternities, founded and directed for the religious orders. Family businesses have left a legacy of economic and philanthropic progress in the regions where they have developed.

Finally, we exemplified two cases of the oldest family businesses in the continent, Grupo Cuervo and Los Lingues, both of which emerged from this process of land granted to the Spaniards through the haciendas or estancias and that are maintained to date. These examples show the importance of the heterogeneity of both companies in their cultures, their relational capital since their foundation and in the strategic business decisions of diversification and growth that the different generations have had to make in order to remain in force.

From this chapter we can reflect on several important learnings for the field of family businesses. To do so, we can take as a reference the importance and performance measurement of family businesses from a historical perspective (Colli A., 2012; Colli A. et al., 2013) concerning issues such as survival through generations, reputation, and social responsibility, as well as the transferability of intangible capital of family businesses. From the point of view of survival, we refer to two cases that are possibly the two longest surviving family business in Latin America and that allow us to reflect on the survival of both, which has had to do with the ability of the different generations to maintain the ownership of the company in the hands of the family and to remain relevant in its value proposition in its different stages. Keeping ownership in the hands of the family has to a large extent to do with having an adequate governance system that would allow them to avoid conflicts among family members and also with maintaining an attitude of stewardship of the patrimony. Another factor may be the inheritance of ownership to a few shareholders, not to all the sons or daughters, from generation to generation, thus reducing complexity and facilitating decision making and ensuring competent leadership in each cycle of the family business. Staying current in the value proposition means innovating, adapting and reformulating its products and services to the needs of different times and taking advantage of existing resources and technologies.

Another important element to reflect on is the reputation and prestige that family businesses achieve. From the pre-Columbian economy to the family economic groups of the colony, we have been able to observe the relevant role of family business and their prestigious position in the social system. Before the arrival of the Spanish and Portuguese, artisans, farmers, and merchants were a privileged class and well valued for their contribution to society. In colonial times, although the privileged position of the landowners and merchants was due to the accumulation and concentration of wealth, in addition to the fact that they were family businesses from the Old World, they managed to imbibe the culture and practices of the community, which is why they became rooted in them and led them to commit themselves and carry out philanthropic activities to compensate in some way for the existing poverty and inequality, which contributed to the prestige of these families in society and many of their donations to hospitals and educational centers are maintained to this day.

The transfer of knowledge, education, and social capital is something that we can also look at as part of the cultural heritage that we have described above and that is part of the heterogeneity of Latin American family businesses. The education of the following generations has to do with the broad definition of family that arises from cultural syncretism. This allows a greater richness in the practices of socialization and collective knowledge that the new generations acquire by the simple fact that they learn from a greater number of people that make up the family nucleus. Social capital, that is, the network of contacts, was fundamental in the development of Latin American family businesses in this period. For example, maintaining an adequate relationship and influence with the political and ecclesiastical power in the colony was essential to maintain and grow family businesses; the same was true of expanding relationships and connections through marriages that could bring together and expand the wealth and patrimony of two wealthy families. It was also very important to maintain ties on both sides of the Atlantic, especially for merchants. All this social capital and knowledge had to be transferred through the generations with effective succession practices and mechanisms.

The first Latin American family businesses are a reflection of the syncretism that took place between the native peoples and the settlers of the Spanish and Portuguese conquest. From this mixture, the political, social, and economic factors that allowed the formation of family businesses in the continent were built and of which, we can be sure, their origin is heterogeneity.

References

Almaraz, A. (2014). De la filantropía colonial a la filantropía globalizada. Una revisión del marco institucional y las prácticas empresariales en México. *Sociedad y Utopía: Revista De Ciencias Sociales, 44*, 73–100.

Bolívar Echeverría. *La clave barroca en América Latina.* Exposition at the Latein-Amerika Institut of the Freie Universität Berlin, November 2002. Published on the website "Bolívar Echeverría: Critical discourse and philosophy of culture".

Colli, A. (2011). Business history in family business studies: From neglect to cooperation? *Journal of Family Business Management.*

Colli, A. (2012). Contextualizing performances of family firms: The perspective of business history. *Family Business Review, 25*(3), 243–257.

Colli, A., Perez, P. F., Melin, L., Nordqvist, M., & Sharma, P. (2013). Business history and family firms. *Sage Handbook of Family Firms, Sage, Londres,* 269–292.

Cruz, E. (2017). Filantropía y donaciones en Chile: Presente, Pasado y Futuro. *Corporación Patrimonio Cultural de Chile.*

Cuervo Tradicional, "Historia de José Cuervo Tradicional". *Cuervo tradicional.* Accessed 2021, http://cuervotradicional.com.mx/#blog.

Dana, L. P. (2015). Indigenous entrepreneurship: An emerging field of research. *International Journal of Business and Globalisation, 14*(2), 158–169.

De Orellana, M. (1999). Microhistoria del tequila: el caso Cuervo. *Artes De México* (27), 28–35. From http://www.jstor.org/stable/24326512.

Economía y Negocios. "Tras fin a la disputa marcaria por Los Lingues, Germán Claro inicia nuevos negocios". *Economía y Negocios*. Accessed 2021, http://www.economiaynegocios.cl/noticias/noticias.asp?id=138126.

El Mercurio. "Las diez empresas familiares vigentes más antiguas de Chile". *El Mercurio*. Ediciones especiales. Accessed 2021, http://www.ediciones especiales.elmercurio.com/destacadas/detalle/index.asp?idnoticia=201009 15496593#:~:text=S.XVII-,Hacienda%20Los%20Lingues,la%20Estancia% 20de%20la%20Angostura.

Escalante Gonzalbo, P. (2004). El México Antiguo en Escalante Gonzalbo, P., García Martínez, B., Jáuregui, L., Zoraida Vázquez, J., Speckman Guerra, E., Garcíadiego, J., & Aboites Aguilar, L. (2004). *Nueva historia mínima de México*. El Colegio de México.

Gimeno, A., Baulenas, G., & Coma-Cros, J. (2010). Family business models. In *Family business models* (pp. 57–77). Palgrave Macmillan.

Hacienda Los Lingues. "Historia y cultura". *Hacienda Los Lingues*. Accessed 2021, https://www.loslingues.com/es-es/historia?page_id=89075#:~:text= Los%20or%C3%ADgenes%20de%20la%20Hacienda%20se%20remo ntan%20a%20fines%20del%20siglo%20XVI.&text=El%20actual%20prop ietario%20de%20Los,%C3%A9poca%20de%20su%20primitiva%20cons trucci%C3%B3n.

Koch, A., Brierley, C., Maslin, M. M., & Lewis, S. L. (2019). Earth system impacts of the European arrival and Great Dying in the Americas after 1492. *Quaternary Science Reviews, 207*, 13–36.

Lafaye, J. (2015). *Quetzalcóatl y Guadalupe: La formación de la conciencia nacional en México: Abismo de conceptos: Identidad, nación, mexicano*. Fondo de cultura económica.

Macpherson, W. G., Tretiakov, A., Mika, J. P., & Felzensztein, C. (2021). Indigenous entrepreneurship: Insights from Chile and New Zealand. *Journal of Business Research, 127*, 77–84.

Manzanilla Naim, L. (2018). *Teotihuacan, ciudad excepcional de Mesoamérica*. El Colegio Nacional.

Molina-Ramírez, E., & Barba-Sánchez, V. (2021). Embeddedness as a differentiating element of indigenous entrepreneurship: Insights from Mexico. *Sustainability, 13*(4), 2117.

Noejovich, H. (1996). *Los albores de la economía en América*. Editorial de la Pontificia Universidad Católica del Perú.

Pekerti, A. A., & Thomas, D. C. (2016). n-Culturals: Modeling the multicultural identity. *Cross Cultural and Strategic Management, 23*(1), 101–127.

Peredo, A. M., Anderson, R. B., Galbraith, C. S., Honig, B., & Dana, L. P. (2004). Towards a theory of indigenous entrepreneurship. *International Journal of Entrepreneurship and Small Business, 1*(1–2), 1–20.

Rautiainen, M., Rosa, P., Pihkala, T., Parada, M. J., & Cruz, A. D. (2019). *The family business group phenomenon.* Springer International Publishing.

Rouquié, A. (1989). América Latina: Introducción al extremo occidente. Siglo XXI.

Singer, P. (1984). Campo y ciudad en el contexto histórico latinoamericano.

Slicher, B. (1992). "Dos modelos referidos a la relación entre población y economía en Nueva España y Perú durante la época colonial". *Empresarios, indios y estado; perfil de la economía mexicana.*

Storey, R., & Widmer, R. (2006). The pre-Columbian economy. *The Cambridge Economic History of Latin America: THe Colonial Era and the Short Nineteenth Century, 1,* 73–105.

Tretiakov, A., Felzensztein, C., Zwerg, A. M., Mika, J. P., & Macpherson, W. G. (2020). Family, community, and globalization: Wayuu indigenous entrepreneurs as n-Culturals. *Cross Cultural & Strategic Management.*

Von Wobeser, G. (1989). La formación de la hacienda en la época colonial. *El uso de la tierra y el agua,* 22.

4

First Migration Flows (the Second Wave): A New Culture of Family Businesses

This section presents the main migration flows that dominated the process of colonization and occupation of Latin America, particularly during its first 250 years, and how these migration flows gradually shaped cultural elements, traditions, beliefs, and practices that are reflected in the diversity and heterogeneity of family businesses in the region.

The different groups of migrants from Asia, Central Europe, Eastern Europe, and Africa brought their own culture, generating a vast amount of knowledge, especially tacit knowledge (Nonaka & Takeuchi, 1995), such as beliefs and values. This process generated an accumulation of intangible resources that shaped the new society. These intangible assets were very different depending on the region from which the migrant came. While this phenomenon has been studied previously, it has not been addressed from a perspective of thoughtful family businesses, their social capital, and business performance (Tata & Prasad, 2015), nor from the perspective of how migration affected the formation of social capital and how it shaped the family business.

C. G. Müller and F. Sandoval-Arzaga, *Family Business Heterogeneity in Latin America*, Palgrave Studies in Family Business Heterogeneity,
https://doi.org/10.1007/978-3-030-78931-2_4

In this section, we include two cases as examples of these phenomena: one of them on the influence of Japanese culture in shaping the characteristics of family businesses in Brazil and another of the Italian migration in Argentina.

Therefore, this chapter provides the reader with the following learning objectives:

- To identify the process of migration flows in the different Latin American countries as a basis for the emergence of family businesses that have driven the region's economy.
- To analyze two successful cases of continuity of Latin American family businesses that survive to this day and which are the product of this period.

4.1   The Migration Flows

Migration has played a critical role in the development of the world, especially in the Americas and particularly in the Latin American region. Because of its recent discovery in 1492, no other region has been made up by migration flows from such different and heterogeneous areas globally in its first 250 years of development. This is one-fifth the time of the entire so-called Middle Ages.

Currently, more than 65% of the population of Latin America descends from migrants. This figure increases to more than 80% if we exclude the regions with the densest concentration of native peoples, such as Bolivia, Peru, Honduras, Guatemala, or southern Mexico (Fig. 4.1).

The fact that no other place in the world besides Australia and New Zealand has such a new population is proof of this.

This foundational condition is reflected in the heterogeneity of family businesses that we can observe in the region. Veider and Matzler (2016) indicate that one of the sources of heterogeneity is the family business's idiosyncratic structure. Based on a study of organizational ambidexterity, the authors mention that family-controlled firms present differences based on their governance structure, resources, and divergent objectives.

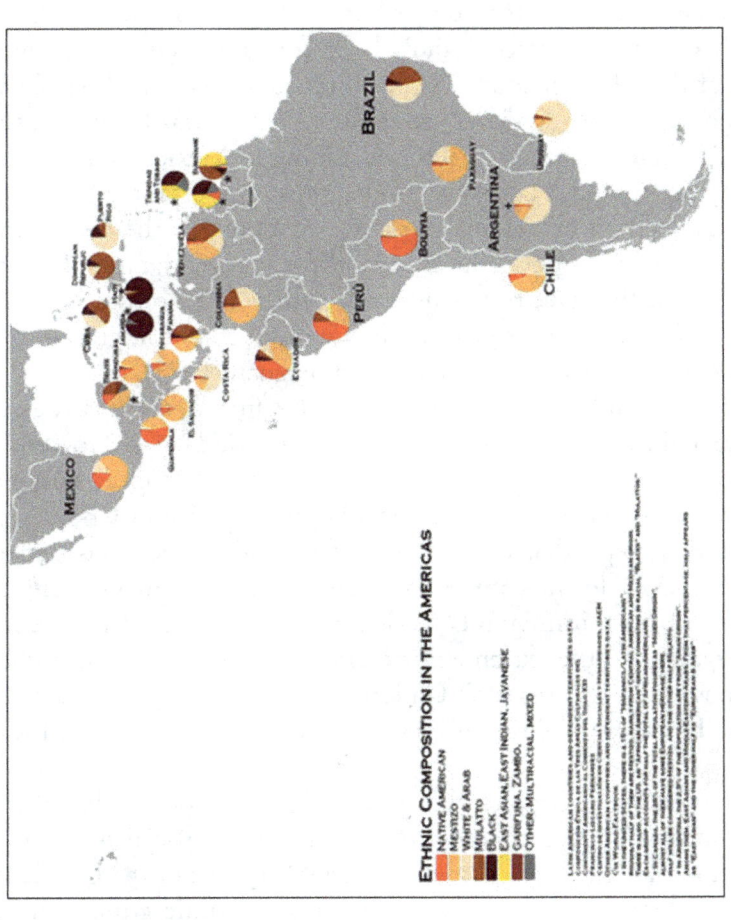

Fig. 4.1 Ethnic composition in Latin America (*Source* Adapted from Peloso [2014])

This behavior, which is reflected in the way of thinking, feeling, and acting, are features of the culture, in our object study, so divergent from its beginnings.

These cultural traits were developed from the first migration flows based on wealth extraction incentives, particularly in Brazil, Mexico, and Peru. Opportunities for gold, silver, and diamond mining in the eighteenth century attracted hundreds of migrants. There are several examples of this phenomenon. In Brazil, the gold rush in Minas Gerais caused a golden age along the entire coast of central Brazil and a massive influx of Portuguese immigrants. Silver mining in Mexico and its transport to Spain turned Havana into the most important port in the Americas to such an extent that a service economy in the seventeenth century made Cuba a powerful attraction for many migrants. In Peru, export, through the river routes developed from 1750 onwards, consequently boosted Argentine's gross domestic product and migration rates above Mexico's or Peru's (Monaghan & Monaghan, 1973).

The case of Chile is more particular; the first Spanish settlers in Chile were mainly soldiers. During the colonial period—1498 to 1800—Spanish legal barriers blocked the migration of other European nationalities. However, in 1700, French settlers began to arrive in Chile. With the country's independence in 1810, a free trade policy was decreed that paved the way for new migration waves. The government promoted German and British immigrants' settlement in the south of the Central Valley, Croatians in the extreme north and south. A significant number of Peruvians and Bolivians took Chilean citizenship with the incorporation of the Tarapacá province into the country after the War of the Pacific in 1879.

As in the previous examples, this varied migration not only had demographic and economic consequences but, above all, social ones in the configuration of future societies and the establishment of the first family businesses. There was little or limited mixing of ethnic groups; on the one hand, the new viruses brought from Europe quickly decimated the indigenous population, in the same manner as the medieval black plague and the Spanish flu pandemic, and on the other, the creation of societies that were very closed in their own culture.

In the following sections, we show some examples of this varied and heterogeneous arrival of people coming not only from Europe but also from Asia and Africa.

4.1.1 Migration from Spain and Portugal

This is the largest group by natural condition since the colonizers were mainly from the kingdoms of Spain and Portugal. In the beginning, when it came to populating America, Spain and Portugal had to rely on servants and convicts as a strategic control measure. Spain restricted migration to America from the outset of the colonization process and Portugal in 1720. The Portuguese used prisoners to settle the regions, but in limited numbers, less than 850 over 70 years, compared to British convicts sent to the United States over a similar period. During the gold rush in Minas Gerais, 900,000 Spaniards and 700,000 Portuguese arrived in the New World in the colonial period. These were single men compared to the more family-oriented migratory movement from North America, where it was populated through settlements composed of English families.

In almost all Central and South America, the urban planning model was based in the Spanish style of a grid pattern with a central square in all founded cities. Moreover, Spanish rule imposed a legal culture that regulated all civic life, from marriage and domestic relations to inheritance and commercial contracts. Roman Catholicism had a lasting effect throughout the region, both as a set of beliefs and practices and as a public institution. The Spanish cultural mark is the main commonality that justifies including countries and regions that are drastically different in racial-ethnic composition.

4.1.2 Other European Regions

Other countries such as France, Italy, and England prompted many people to relocate to the colonies and ended up engaging in various forms of forced or semi-voluntary migrations or displacement. More than 400,000 Englishmen who came to the New World before 1780 did so as indentured servants and more than 50,000 as convicts. In some cases, there was a greater concentration from specific regions of a country as in Italy, where the most significant number of migrants came from the Lombardy region. Migration from other regions of Europe besides Spain took on enormous dimensions in the United States well before Latin America. One exception was the Italian migration to South America, which reached large numbers earlier than in the United States. In 1900, the Italian community in Buenos Aires, Argentina, was more significant than in the top ten populous Italian migrant cities in the United States combined. The fact that the South American migrants came from Italy's upper fringe gave these early Italian settlements in Latin America a strong character with their distinct traditions, cuisine, and social interaction.

4.1.3 Central Europe, Eastern Europe, and the Middle East

Although to a lesser extent, there was a migration of Eastern Europeans. Argentina recorded an influx of 180,000 Poles and 48,000 Yugoslavians after World War I. In the early 1890s, the Brazilian gold rush brought thousands of Polish peasants to Brazil; an American geographer estimated that 240,000 of them resided in the three southernmost Brazilian states. Palestinians, meanwhile, accounted for 2% of the population in Honduras. The same happened in Ecuador with migrants of Lebanese origin (Moya, 2018).

Many of the 340,000 Middle Eastern migrants who arrived in Latin America settled mainly in Argentina and Brazil and were registered with Turkish nationality because they traveled with Ottoman passports. However, few were Turks or even Muslims. The vast majority were from other religious minorities in the Ottoman Empire or were of Jewish descent. Armenians, scattered throughout the Middle East, came from a variety of countries.

4.1.4 Africa and Asia

Between 1492 and the mid-nineteenth century, the number of people traveling from Africa to the Americas exceeded the migration from Europe four times. During the first period of colonization in the sixteenth century, 45% of African migrants arrived in Brazil. This number increased after the Haitian Revolution and the abolition of the slave trade by the British Empire in 1807. Latin America became the leading destination of African migrants, receiving 88% of all African slaves during the nineteenth century. Up until the abolishment of slavery in the late 1890s, there were 35,000 slave ship voyages .from Africa, and—according to many historians—this represented the first genuinely massive transoceanic movement in the history of humankind.

A significant wave of migrants came from Asia. The importation of Asian migrant workers to the European colonies in America occurred in the seventeenth century. However, in the nineteenth century, the so-called coolie trade (laborers from China mainly) developed, in response to the African slave trade and the end of slavery, as the preferred mode of labor for many plantation owners. The first Chinese workers arrived in the colony of Trinidad—now Trinidad and Tobago in the Caribbean—in the 1800s. In South America, Chinese indentured laborers worked in the silver mines and coastal industries of Peru, accounting for more than 100,000 Chinese migrants as indentured laborers. During the 1800s, many Indian migrants voluntarily enlisted to go abroad to work. European traders quickly took advantage of this and began to recruit them to work as a source of cheap labor. A notable difference between the Chinese coolies and the Indian migrants was that men, women, and children were brought from India, while the Chinese coolies were 99% male. This led to a high rate of Chinese men marrying women of other ethnicities, such as native women and mixed-race Creole women. Some 580,000 Asians arrived in Latin America before World War II. More than 360,000 were Chinese and settled in Cuba, Peru, and northern Mexico. The established Chinese communities were still relatively small. The Japanese arrived later, but as family groups, and despite their small numbers, the ethnic communities grew much faster. The Japanese population in Brazil migration is currently 2 million, resulting in the largest group outside Japan.

As shown in the previous paragraphs, the migration flow settlements developed differently over time, particularly between 1492 and the early 1800s. Both in terms of intensity and quantity, they depended essentially on the historical circumstances of the different policies promoted from Europe.

Servants, convicts, and free men were a majority and heterogeneous group within the first settlements of the first massive colonizing groups in this region. Displaced people from Africa were another relevant and constant group in flux compared to other ethnic groups or regions of migrants where the promise of a better life prevailed as an incentive to colonize and establish the first societies. On the other hand, Spain's influence is reflected not only in the language and the religion but also in the social interaction and customs, as seen in the city planning, which included a central plaza in all the founded cities.

This has had enormous implications in how family businesses have evolved in the different regions of Latin America. One such reflection is the establishment of the values of entrepreneurial spirit. Much of North America was colonized from England with families that made the settlements, and their sense of entrepreneurship was collective. This meant that not just individual effort or talent was given priority, but rather optimizing the collective as a whole and entrepreneurship activity based on teamwork and joint effort. It was quite different for Latin America because the first settlers acted as individual entrepreneurs, without family support, and far from their land and with little assistance. Many of these practices may well have been in the interest of extracting wealth instead of colonizing. On the contrary, settlers forced to come to a new land, as in the case of forced migrations from Africa or Asia, lacked the freedom to be masters of their own destiny.

4.2   From the Diaspora to the Enclave

The arrival of these migratory communities gave shape to the establishment of enclaves, geographically delimited places within the emerging cities, in which people of similar nationalities, customs, and traditions settled down. This type of clusters was organized to carry out their lives far from their land, but with elements such as music, food, and games of their customs, generating a new rich, and varied culture, especially in regions that were very attractive to the first colonizers who settled in Cuba, southern Mexico, Peru, Brazil, and Argentina.

Other researches indicate a fast integration of migrants in each of the geographical areas where they settled. The fact that by the third generation, many of these groups had already lost their mother tongue, acquiring Spanish or Portuguese very quickly compared to other migrant regions, suggests that the host societies have proven to be steamrollers (Blauner, 1969). Another example is the Yiddish language, which had survived for a millennium as the language of ethnic minorities in Central and Eastern Europe. After three generations, migrants of Jewish origin and had settled in Argentina, Uruguay and Brazil, had already lost their native tongue, replacing it with the host country's language. Other studies indicate that more than half of the Jews in Argentina, Uruguay, Brazil, and the United States marry outside the group, an unprecedented level in the history of a group whose exogamy rates in Eastern Europe, North Africa, and the Middle East around 1930 were below 2%. Today's rates are below 35% in other diasporas such as Australia, Canada, and New Zealand and less than 25% in South Africa.

This generation of local communities was remarkably different in Latin America: they maintained many of their diaspora traditions and culture, adapted to the language, adopted the local religion, and created networks. Indeed, they are the first locals of the world (Robertson, 1995).

4.3   Migrant Family Businesses and Their Social Capital

Hanifan (1916) described that the intangible assets that count most in people's daily lives are: knowledge, willingness, companionship, sympathy, and social relationships between individuals and families that form a social unit. Latin America's social capital was built from the fabric of many relationships and shared values that may be unique to family relationships. Social capital is inherent in most family businesses by virtue of the basis of a family unit.

Management and economics distinguish several categories of capital that describe the different resources a community or organization has access to. These resources are accessible to individuals or companies and can be applied to the production of goods and services. Since none of the aforementioned encompasses the uniqueness of human beings, nor their capabilities or relationships, the classification of resources is complemented by human capital, that is, capabilities and knowledge, and social capital, which refers to relational structures.

There is a wide variety of definitions that attempt to account for the concept of social capital. Among these, Coleman (1988), from a more sociological perspective, defines social capital as those consistent aspects of social structure, obligations and expectations, information channels, sets of norms, and sanction systems, which constrain or encourage socially and economically constructive behaviors.

In the family business case, the business itself is a network, as is the family. In turn, both have a wider network than that made up of the members of a community. When family and company are mixed, two notably different network models interact. Thus, for example, the family ties make it possible to transcend those of the organization itself, generating more profound and more extensive links and guaranteeing their transferability across generations. As Gersick et al. (1999) a family business culture associated with a history provides a special meaning to the activity carried out. Family members and other business members share visions of how the business should operate and what rules should be respected.

If we view these social capital creation principles through the first migration flows lens, we undoubtedly have a comprehensive source of heterogeneity. It has also been argued that social capital formation is founded not only in terms of culture, religion, traditions, or narratives but within collectives through cooperation, trust, and cohesion (Nahapiet & Ghoshal, 1998).

The process associated with the creation of social capital is linked to these structural components—a sense of belonging, security, and cohesion—when family members interact with business roles—formal or informal—can leverage their own family ties and build relationships with their employers for the benefit of the family business (Arregle et al., 2007). This ability to leverage the family structure to benefit the organization indicates a concept known as appropriation, namely, how relationships in one social structure can be transferred to another structure—family and firm and vice versa (Coleman, 1988).

The foundation of the first families under these migration flows is unquestionably a source of social capital creation, laying the grounds for moral behavior and cooperation. The family is an institution that contributes to shaping its members' attitudes and behaviors and, consequently, has an apparent effect on the generation of the family business's social capital. The family and the company spread—among the individuals that constitute it—shared visions and norms that must be respected. These behaviors promote the emergence of cooperative initiatives and mutually beneficial collective actions (Kwon & Adler, 2014). In this way, the group and diversity brought by the different migration flows to Latin America generated a social capital linked to the generation of shared values that were the basis for future behavior. These value backgrounds are based on family history and culture (Carr et al., 2011).

4.4 Next Generations: First Economic Groups of Migrant Families

The first unforced migrants were initially motivated by the extraction of gold and silver from different Latin American regions. The cities that were founded around these mining deposits became a major pillar of the economy during this period, strongly influencing the population's social life. That is why the Crown of Spain and Portugal were responsible for protecting all types of mining operations, mainly gold and silver, not only because of what it meant for the community but also because of the 20% tribute payment for these activities.

At the same time, there was a phenomenon of exportation from America to Europe of various crops that the colonizers were incorporating into their diet, which implied a transfer of plants from one area to another. This enriched a food supply that was increased with the incorporation of species transplanted from Europe. In this way, products such as corn, beans, cocoa, pineapples, and avocados began to be traded from America to Europe. These first commercial initiatives gave birth to the earliest entrepreneurs who began developing, processing, and exporting various semi-finished agricultural products with the local authorities' sponsorship. Tallow and leather were other types of products of significant consumption and demand, the former being the raw material used in the elaboration of candles.

The kingdoms of Spain and Portugal established a commercial monopoly with America. They implemented a fleet system and galleons, which consisted of the circulation of merchant ships from Europe to America and vice versa, which carried raw materials and manufactured products to be traded. These were closely watched by warships, which ensured the integrity of the goods and the crew. As a result, the exchange was constant, and the first entrepreneurs and merchants traded in the region of Portobello (currently Panama) to acquire manufactured products from Europe, including arms, jewelry, oil, wine, and fabrics. The commercial monopoly was so strict that even the exchange between the colonies was strongly supervised. Surveillance was gradually changed when Spain's regulations made trade restrictions more flexible in the seventeenth century. One of them directly impacted commercial growth since it allowed the opening of essential ports and trade development as we know it today. Despite this progressive entrepreneurial freedom, Spain's trade administration was subjected to the payment of taxes levied on various exports. Among them were the *quinto real*, which taxed gold, the *almojarifazgo*, a customs tax on goods that circulated between Spain and America, the *alcabala*, related to the purchase and sale of movable and immovable goods, and the *anata*, corresponding to the payment of one or half a year's salary.

The expansion of trade for local consumption was also important, less subjected to taxes, which generated local economies' development based on agricultural and consumer products. On the other hand, the arrival of different traders from Europe, such as apothecaries, locksmiths, carvers, tailors, bakers, musicians, blacksmiths, smelters, and scribes, gave life to the first budding industrial settlements. This more primitive type of industry arose spontaneously where there was a market for an article without external supply or, in many cases, through smuggling. Industrial development, then, is the response to the lack of initiative of the Kingdom of Spain or Portugal in supplying their colonies with manufactured products. In general, in the most developed settlements of its time, the craft industry reached great importance in cities, and it was oriented at producing daily demand articles, highlighting the activities related to clothing, such as tailors, shoemakers, embroiderers; food products like bread, cheese, sugar, and honey; and artistic crafts, especially gold and silversmithing.

Foundries or industries related to livestock farming, such as leather tanning, tallow candles, soap, or construction, such as bricks or transportation (manufacture of carts), also developed. However, besides these artisanal activities, the first major Latin American industries were textile manufacturing and shipbuilding. The shipbuilding industry was favored by the abundance of raw materials, such as wood, cotton, and pita fiber for sails and cordage, tar for caulking, and other necessary materials, except for iron, which had to be imported from Spain. The shipyards of Havana and Guayaquil in Ecuador stand out above all.

Thus, we see three types of enterprising families of the sixteenth century, those migrants of Spanish or Portuguese origin who obtained a permit to cultivate the land—*encomenderos*—and other migrants of diverse origins who, by means of a trade, managed to make their way into society producing goods or services, and the third group of merchants who were familiar with the foreign trade system of the time.

The birth of families that followed one generation after another in developing a specific economic activity always had a prevalence of family ties and the creation of robust political and social networks both with the monarchy that administered the laws and among the local families themselves.

4.5 Case Studies

4.5.1 Dimare Family, Rusti Company—Argentina

The migration of people from Italy began early in 1550 through individual initiatives—clergymen, military, and entrepreneurs—but was very limited due to the existing regulations in the first years of colonization. Nevertheless, it was not until 1700 that, together with the expansion of commercial traffic to the area of the Rio de la Plata—nowadays Buenos Aires—, a flow of migration began in response to the demand for specific trades such as craftsmen and builders as well as the opportunities offered by this vast region. Doménico Belgrano's case illustrates the importance of Italian belonging and identity in the nascent Argentine society. He was a Genoese merchant, who integrated into the local society, started a family, and became firmly rooted in the civil society. Later, one of his sons, Manuel Belgrano, a lawyer, politician, and military man, became one of the key figures in the process that led to Argentina's independence. As in many other cases, second-generation migrants already took on local identity and adhered to the social space.

However, it was not until the mid-1800s, with the promotion of migration policies, that a massive flow took place. Between 1870 and 1920, Argentina received about 6 million migrants from various Italian regions, mainly Genoa.

The extent of this movement is decisive in Argentina's demographic history. From 1.7 million inhabitants in 1869, the population grew to more than 7.8 million in 1914. The foreign population's relative weight more than doubled from 12% to more than 30% in 1914.

Along with hundreds of similar migration cases is the one of Antonio Dimare, who traveled from Italy when he was 14 years old in 1957. He arrived in Buenos Aires on the Conte Biancamano ship that had sailed from Naples 20 days earlier. He traveled with his mother, Teresa, his father, Cataldo, and his brothers, José and Alfredo; his sister, Sisina, had already migrated a year before. Then he started working in a grocery store, and on weekends he sold fresh pasta on the streets of the neighborhood to earn some extra money. One day he decided to become economically independent and thought of buying a pasta factory, but when he arrived at the place where they offered such a machine with the classified ads from the newspaper in one hand and a handful of optimism in the other, the factory was closed, and he had to change course.

In alphabetical order, after pasta came plastics. He walked a little further and came to a small company called Barr, a rustic workshop where they manufactured plastic parts with minimal complexity. He and his brothers put together their savings and bought the place. However, he immediately decided to shift the factory to a niche he saw as promising: didactic toys.

"The key to our family business is sharing the vision and working together," explains Gabriel Dimare, commercial director and fourth son of the founder. "We have to respect each other a lot, even if we don't always agree on everything. Our father was the one who taught us to respect each other day by day, and he was with us when we wanted to innovate and never left us alone."

The second generation of the Dimare Family is led by five siblings; the company has 100 employees, and more than 50 years of experience. The family places great emphasis on nurturing family relationships and how the different generations have worked together smoothly without clashing in the attempt.

When the second generation was still infant, the five siblings: Daniel, Fabián, Sergio, Gabriel, and Sabrina, had fun with the educational toys made by Antonio, but they also had other entertainment. "We would play at being office workers with old papers from the workshop," says Gabriel. He adds: "When our father came back from the plant, he never complained about his work. He always enjoyed it and the factory, to this day, is his life." During the summers, Gabriel would go to the factory, and his father would teach him the trade and make him work and learn about the business, along with going with him to make deliveries, collections, or preparation of orders. "Since the trade is fun, I never thought of working in anything else. My brothers and I got into the family business of our own accord" says Gabriel.

This is how they have faced the challenges of the local economy. The company has had three stages: between 1965 and 1991, it was the stage of foundation, effort, and intuition, in which only domestic production was manufactured; then from 1991 to 2001, there was a strictly importing period; and since 2003, the focus has been on brand management.

During the first stage, the founder established himself as a plastic toy manufacturer, acquired another plant with its machinery and tooling, and created new lines. Nevertheless, he was fascinated by one in particular: the German brand Rasti. Gabriel says that during the 1970s, there was a rumor that the company might be for sale. His father dreamed of becoming the owner. At the same time, the local market was demanding imported products and the opportunity for him was clear: he had to buy the brand. "Financially, it was impossible. But he did not give up: he developed another brand inspired by the competition, called Plastiblock, also of small plastic bricks, and he did very well and went through the economic downturn of 1976. He saw this as a great opportunity that led him to get out of the comfort zone and encouraged him to do more," Gabriel comments.

In 1984, the company started an export process. It achieved a relevant position in the local market and began shipping to the United States, England, Israel, Mexico, Brazil, Morocco, and South Africa. In 1990 it was selling up to 35% of its production abroad. In 1991 Dimare traveled to China in search of parts to include in his domestic products. "He discovered that everything was cheap there and had to put aside his love for manufacturing and became an importer," he recounted. "The 1990s made us all forget about manufacturing. The company grew a lot, and it was another opportunity," indicates Gabriel.

After the devaluation of the Argentine peso and financial crisis in 2002, the company was reborn: it started manufacturing again, but this time it included brand management among its priorities.

In 2008, they certified ISO 9001 standards, which unify production processes and commit to continuous improvement. "We were the first toy factory in the country to do so. It is very important; it is a commitment that we wanted to make, besides the fact that it gives us prestige and allows us to be in all the main chains in the country," explained Dimare.

In 2011, the Dimare family agreed to a family protocol in which conflict prevention rules were established to ensure the company's continuity as new generations were incorporated. They also made a deal with Mattel, which offered them the exclusive distribution of Rasti and Blocky in Colombia, Peru, Mexico, and Chile. Additionally, since 2012, the company has a 9000 square meter plant.

"Our exports are less than 10% of our business, and we do them out of love for our country since they do not generate a significant income. We believe that there is great potential, but the current situation is not ideal. We are betting that at some point, it will be reversed, although we are aware that we will never be able to compete in production and prices with China," Gabriel points out.

Gabriel Dimare has a four-year-old son, and, according to him, the only toys his son has fun with are blocks. "And that's the way I can build things for him and be his hero," he joked. Passion is passed down from generation to generation; Antonio, the founder, is 72 years old and still goes to the factory every day. "My father has always worked. He comes to accompany us, he is not looking for anything else, but the factory is his life," concluded Gabriel, trustee, and heir to the legacy.

4.5.2 Nishimura Family, Jacto—Brazil

Japanese migration in Brazil occurred later than other Latin American flows, but no less significant in its cultural roots and impact upon the family business mark. As we have already seen in previous sections, the Asian immigrants came mainly from China and India, where many performed forced labor with poor working conditions and bordering on slavery. This flow of migrants had its beginning in the late 1800s, but it is particularly interesting because of the legendary Japanese past, which is entirely different from Brazil's western culture.

According to Cintra (1971), Japanese migration to Brazil had an initial goal of relocating the increasing population the country was facing in the mid-1850s. To this end, the Japanese government promoted migration by financing part of the transfer, particularly to Sao Paulo, where it signed cooperation agreements to work on coffee farms. However, a second objective was to incorporate the Japanese private sector as a stakeholder in promoting and subsidizing groups of citizens wishing to migrate to Brazil. Thus, Japan developed a strategy to ensure the supply of raw materials. The Japanese interests envisioned Brazil as something more than a mere territory that could solve the population problems. Following England's example, which controlled the foreign trade of coffee through the São Paulo Railway Company, Japanese industrialists initiated a broad policy of investments—mainly in the agricultural sector. Organized as institutions in which capital and labor were purely Japanese, these companies were destined to play the role of authentic enclaves of the Japanese economy in Brazilian territory.

One hundred years later in Brazil, we can find an estimated of 2 million Japanese descendants in Sao Paulo alone, whose influence on society has extended from farmland to martial arts, architecture, and business.

Third and fourth-generation family businesses of Japanese origin in Brazil have married with African descendants, Italians, and Portuguese. Some of them have returned to Japan in a wave of reverse migration, often saying that the Japanese treat them as foreigners. After years of hard work on coffee farms, Japanese immigrants sought work in big cities like Sao Paulo, where they flocked to the city center because the rent was cheaper. The Liberdade district in downtown Sao Paulo is a slice of Tokyo, its main street lined with red torii gates from Shinto shrines. Sushi restaurants compete with karaoke bars.

The young Japanese Shunji Nishimura case represents this wave of migration and how they turned into unique family businesses while maintaining their tradition. Nishimura decided to leave Japan in 1932 to work in Brazil. Like other migrants, his goal was to earn money quickly and return to Kyoto, his hometown. Thousands of other Japanese migrants had made the same journey before him to Brazilian coffee plantations where they had the prospect of a better life. For 22-year-old

Nishimura, at that time, it was all different. "One of the things they used to tell people that attracted them here is that in Brazil, you could find money hanging on trees," says Jorge Nishimura, who is second generation in the company. The family lives in a remote village in the state of Sao Paulo, now running a company with 4500 employees built on Shunji Nishimura's invention of a machine to spray pesticides on crops, an example of the strong Japanese influence on farming techniques.

Nishimura was part of the wave of Japanese migration when Brazil had abolished slavery and needed workers for coffee plantations to boost its economy, while industrialized Japan had a surplus of peasants.

Within weeks of his arrival in Brazil, young Shunji began harvesting coffee on the Santa Maria farm in the town of Botucatu. The work was hard, and the pay was small. Eventually, Shunji decided to go to Rio de Janeiro, where he worked as a butler for a couple in Petrópolis. He saved some money with the intention of resuming his studies, improving his Portuguese, getting to know Brazil, and exploring its opportunities.

In 1934 he returned to São Paulo and enrolled in elementary school. He studied eight hours a day and worked at the school. A year later, he ran out of money. He left school and found work as a lathe operator and welder in a factory. The salary was so low that sometimes he only had bread and banana for breakfast. At the Brazilian Episcopal Church, he met his wife, Chieko Suzukayama. In 1939 Shunji decided to try his luck in the countryside. He took a train from São Paulo to the Alta Paulista region and then got off 472 km at the last stop: Pompéia, at that time, was a small village of wooden houses, currently Pompéia is the Headquarters of Jacto Group. Shunji Nishimura rented a house and hung a sign that read, "We fix everything." He fixed bowls, transformed lubricant oil cans into buckets and jugs, invented an alembic for distilling menthol, fixed farm machinery, and trucks, adapted gasoline engines to gas, among other things. In this workshop, farmers also asked Nishimura to fix their imported agrochemical sprinklers, which had no technical assistance in the region. By fixing so many of them, he designed a new model that was better and easier to use. It was the first sprinkler created in Brazil and the first product of the Jacto brand in 1948. Shunji Nishimura ran Jacto Agricultural Machines until 1972, when the company formed its first board of directors, and his son, Jiro Nishimura, was elected president. The founder then turned his attention to designing new products, such as the first coffee harvester. He continued to guide the company's strategies and decisions. Nishimura died in April 2010 at the age of 99.

4.6   Chapter Summary

From the perspective of migration flows, the Latin American region is the most heterogeneous in the world. The lack of linguistic, religious, and sectarian diversity facilitated the construction of local cultures. This, in turn, explains two paradoxes. By far, the most multiracial region in the world is also the least multicultural and has the most significant racial inequalities. It is also the one with the lowest levels of ethnic and sectarian separatism. Because of this multiracialism, early family businesses were more culturally homogeneous than in most other places as they sought their own identity. The Dimare family in Argentina and the Nishimura family in Brazil show how these early migrants managed to adapt, emerge, and leave a legacy in their territory.

But beyond the arrival of the first settlers such as the Dimare and Nishimura families, all migration flows occurred in the context of the indigenous population, more than 15 different ethnic groups lived in the region. These migration flows had to deal with the political and military influence of the Inca Empire, in the Andean region, for example. After the conquest, most of these groups were assimilated in a short time, becoming the main labor force of the colonial economy. During the colonial period, Spanish legal barriers blocked the migration of other European nationalities. It took 200 years before independence was decreed a free trade policy that opened the way for new waves of immigration from England, North America, and Italy.

Lee's (1966) migration model explain the push and pull factors of migration in most of the processes that were carried out in Latin America, particularly in the two cases presented. A push factor—of Lee's Model—, is somewhat unfavorable in a region in which someone experiences the desire to migrate, the conditions in both Japan and Italy in the late 1890s were decisive for undertaking the adventure of colonizing the new world. The actors of attraction were the best economic conditions that these regions experienced, as well as the cultural and community elements that these regions offered to the settlers.

This section we expected to show that migrations from the various historical periods in which they were executed, such as: conquest, colonialism, slavery, free mass movements, and global diasporas; represent one of the central axes is in the historical formation of family businesses in Latin America. This process explains why this region is the most multiracial and heterogeneous society. Undoubtedly, this phenomenon materialized from movements embodied in structures of great disparities of power, such as the forced migration of slaves. It also explains why those regions of Latin America where the conquest of the native peoples predominated have high levels of social inequality, on the contrary, in others Latin American regions where new settlements based on free migration were developed, have historically had some of the most egalitarian social structures and the highest levels of social mobility. We also showed that the lack of linguistic and religious diversity— Spanish language and Catholic religion—made it easier for post-colonial republics to build national cultures to which the settlers quickly assimilated the local culture. This explains a main paradox: Latin America is the most multiracial region in the world, but also the one with the least cultural diversity based on its migrations.

Certainly, migration flows have been decisive in the explanation of heterogeneity in family businesses in Latin America.

References

Arregle, J. L., Hitt, M. A., Sirmon, D. G., & Very, P. (2007). The development of organizational social capital: Attributes of family firms. *Journal of Management Studies, 44*(1), 73–95.

Blauner, R. (1969). Internal colonialism and ghetto revolt. *Social Problems, 16*(4), 393–408.

Carr, J. C., Cole, M. S., Ring, J. K., & Blettner, D. P. (2011). A measure of variations in internal social capital among family firms. *Entrepreneurship Theory and Practice, 35*(6), 1207–1227.

Cintra, J. T. (1971). *La migración japonesa en Brasil (1908–1958).* El Colegio de México, México.

Coleman, J. S. (1988). Social capital in the creation of human capital. *American Journal of Sociology, 94*, S95–S120.

Gersick, K. E., Lansberg, I., Desjardins, M., & Dunn, B. (1999). Stages and transitions: Managing change in the family business. *Family Business Review, 12*(4), 287–297.

Hanifan, L. J. (1916). The rural school community center. *The Annals of the American Academy of Political and Social Science, 67*(1), 130–138.

Kwon, S. W., & Adler, P. S. (2014). Social capital: Maturation of a field of research. *Academy of Management Review, 39*(4), 412–422.

Lee, E. (1966). A theory of migration. *Demography, 3*(1), 47–57. https://doi.org/10.2307/2060063.

Monaghan, J., & Monaghan, J. (1973). *Chile, Peru, and the California gold rush of 1849.* University of California Press.

Moya, J. (2018). Migration and the historical formation of Latin America in a global perspective. *Sociologias, 20*(49), 24–68.

Nahapiet, J., & Ghoshal, S. (1998). Social capital, intellectual capital, and the organizational advantage. *Academy of Management Review, 23*(2), 242–266.

Nonaka, I., & Takeuchi, H. (1995). *The knowledge-creating company: How Japanese companies create the dynamics of innovation.* Oxford University Press.

Peloso, V. (2014). *Race and ethnicity in Latin American history.* Routledge.

Robertson, R. (1995). Glocalization: Time–space and homogeneity–heterogeneity. In M. Featherstone, S. Lash, & R. Robertson (Eds.), *Global modernities* (pp. 25–44). Sage.

Tata, J., & Prasad, S. (2015). Immigrant family businesses: Social capital, network benefits and business performance. *International Journal of Entrepreneurial Behaviour & Research, 21*(6), 842.

Veider, V., & Matzler, K. (2016). The ability and willingness of family-controlled firms to arrive at organizational ambidexterity. *Journal of Family Business Strategy, 7*(2), 105–116.

5

The Emergence of the Family Group (the Third Wave): From State-Owned Companies to Large Family Groups

This section presents the development of family businesses in Latin America and the sources of heterogeneity from the analysis, creation, and development of prominent Latin American family conglomerates or "grupos económicos" in Spanish (Benavente et al. 1997). This area has been studied from an economic, sociological and, more recently, family business dynamics perspective.

The recent publication by Rautiainen et al. (2019) indicates that family-owned economic groups are even more complex than the traditional multi-divisional form of corporate organization. Additionally, it states that this type of conglomerate is more prevalent in developing countries as regulatory and legal institutions are inadequate, encouraging the risk dilution through smaller legally independent companies.

A similar conclusion is reached by Carney et al. (2018), indicating that the two most common perspectives on the fostering and proliferation of economic clusters are generated by institutional vacuums and entrenchment/exploitation in their industry sector. In fact, these authors suggest that the state's inability to create institutions and the capacity of business groups to adapt to institutions encourage this type of organization.

© The Author(s), under exclusive license to Springer Nature
Switzerland AG 2021
C. G. Müller and F. Sandoval-Arzaga, *Family Business Heterogeneity in Latin America*, Palgrave Studies in Family Business Heterogeneity,
https://doi.org/10.1007/978-3-030-78931-2_5

Learning objectives:

- To map large family groups that emerged as part of a privatization process in Latin America and their link with political power.
- To analyze two successful cases of continuity of Latin American family businesses that have survived until today and are the product of this period.

5.1   Latin American Institutional Environment

The study of the institutional environment has taken on great relevance, especially since 1990 onwards, particularly with North (1999) and Weingast (1993). However, it has been a relevant variable for the exercise of economic transactions in recent centuries, as reflected in the work of Greif (1994: 944) on the merchants of Genoa, Italy, in the twelfth century. In it, they indicated that "it is misleading to expect that a beneficial organization in one society will yield the same results in another," arguing that as early as medieval times, there was a strong notion that trading in one or another society would have different effects with the same resources invested, depending on the political and legal system prevailing in that society.

The study of institutions as determinants of individual behaviors that influence the performance of the economy focuses on the comprehending of societies and their economic systems based on what North (1990) called the "rules of the game," that is, those that define and limit the set of choices that individuals must make decisions.

The concept of institution in the economic domain is identified as the constraints that arise from human resourcefulness to limit political, economic, and social interactions. These constraints include informal ones, which are formed by individuals' daily interaction within a society, which—in turn—determine the direction or foundations of culture, traditions, beliefs, and codes of conduct that do not require formalism to be effective. On the other hand, formal rules require procedures that must be written down on paper, such as laws, constitutions, and property rights, among others.

Thus, any change in institutions, that is, in the rules of the game, directly impacts the transaction costs that will determine the exchanges that may or may not be carried out in accordance with the possibility of increasing wealth as a result. In this regard, any alteration to institutions can become a determining factor in a country's growth and development.

In developed markets such as the countries in the Nordic region of Europe—Norway, Finland, Sweden, Denmark—and others such as Switzerland, Singapore, the Netherlands, and New Zealand, the institutional context is characterized by well-functioning capital markets, labor markets, and access to supplies. The structure and regulation of these markets allow addressing information asymmetries and agency problems, enabling entrepreneurs to raise capital, access management talent, and gain customer acceptance and trust, competing according to the rules of the game. Indeed, in the face of disputes, you can sue for the protection of property rights that the legal environment confers on its business activity.

In emerging markets such as Latin America, there are a variety of market failures caused by information and agency problems. For example, financial markets are characterized by inadequate disclosure and weak government and corporate control. Intermediaries such as financial analysts, investment banks, venture capital agencies, and the financial press are absent or not fully evolved. Securities regulations are generally weak, and enforcement is inconsistent. Information asymmetries between a manager and an employee regarding the value of their human capital, coupled with the absence of training in business schools and certification agencies, can lead to severe flaws in economic models.

Scott (1995) presents a synthetic definition of the institutional environment, the three distinctive pillars of the institutional environment, enforce how individuals and organizations are conformed through implementation of coercive, normative, and mimetic processes. According to North (2002), the absence of a legal framework imposes high transaction costs on entrepreneurs, forcing them to seek short-term benefits that maximize returns and accelerate the investment return. This short-term vision may be an explanation of speculation and the processes of overexploitation of natural resources, and excessive demand on the labor force.

A concrete way of establishing the effects of the institutional environment has been the work of Sobel (2008), using the theory of productive and unproductive entrepreneurship (Baumol, 1990), he verifies the hypothesis that entrepreneurs channel their effort in different directions depending on the quality of the prevailing institutions and laws. This institutional structure determines the reward of investing in productive activities, such as business creation, versus unproductive political and legal activities, such as lobbying and lawsuits. Good institutions— those of higher institutional quality—drive efforts toward productive entrepreneurship, sustaining higher rates of economic growth.

In the context of Latin American institutional environment, we can indicate that there is little applied research (Camargo, 2021; Stosberg, 2018). We replicated Sobel's (2008) study to Latin America, calculating a net entrepreneurship rate, which by definition is equal to the sum of the effective entrepreneurship rate minus the unproductive entrepreneurship rate (Sobel, 2008). An inherent problem with this type of estimation is the non-existence of variables for the phenomena to be analyzed: institutional quality, and productive and unproductive entrepreneurship. However, it is possible to find variables and indicators that approximately represent the objects of study. Although it has obvious limitations, this approach is accepted within the academic community and is thus a good alternative for statistical validation. As a proxy for institutional quality, we used the economic freedom indicator, calculated annually by The Heritage Foundation,[1] covering 186 countries.

For productive entrepreneurship, recognized as those activities with high innovative content and, therefore, which generate value, six proxy variables were used: high-technology exports, research and development expenditure, global innovation index, number of patents per million inhabitants, availability of venture capital, and innovation capacity. The variables were obtained from World Bank, World Intellectual Property Organization, and World Economic Forum records (Table 5.1).

---

[1] https://www.heritage.org/index/.

Table 5.1 Ranking of net entrepreneurship in Latin America

World Rank	Latin American Rank	Country
28	1	Chile
38	2	Uruguay
39	3	Costa Rica
46	4	Brasil
58	5	Panama
60	6	Colombia
61	7	Trinidad y Tobago
62	8	Mexico
63	9	Peru
72	10	Guatemala
75	11	Argentina
79	12	Honduras
85	13	Ecuador
86	14	Paraguay

Source Compiled by authors with data from the World Bank, the World Intellectual Property Organization, the World Economic Forum, and Transparency International (2017–2019)

As proxy variables for unproductive entrepreneurship, the judicial independence index, the irregular payments index, and the corruption perception index were selected. These variables were obtained from the World Economic Forum and Transparency International. All data are part of a panel between 2017 and 2019; the sample has included 86 nations across world regions, including 14 from Latin America.

At the Latin American level, the best ranked in terms of net entrepreneurship rate is Chile scoring 21.92 points in the 28th position worldwide, followed by Uruguay in the 38th position with 2.92 points.

These findings confirm the assumptions that the Latin American institutional environment is low compared to other regions, like countries in the sub-Saharan African region. The majority -8 out of 14- of the countries in this sample is in the lowest percentile of the study. What this indicates is not only the low quality of institutions but also an incentive to the informal economy, contributing to the formation of a culture and codes of conduct, in many cases, outside the legal frameworks.

Furthermore, only three out of the 14 economies studied have a positive rate of entrepreneurship; that is, 11 countries in the study— corresponding to 58% of Latin American countries—could be classified as destructive entrepreneurship economies (Baumol, 1990), as can be seen in Fig. 5.1.

The above is in line with research such as that of Gedajlovic et al. (2012), which states that institutional conditions moderate performance differences between family businesses. More specifically, they suggest adverse effects of institutional conditions experienced by family firms when they are in an emerging economy.

Linked to this is that family firms have a greater capacity to overcome institutional vacuums in emerging economies. In such scenarios, family networks help in market development through cooperation among small firms. Nevertheless, Gedajlovic et al. (2012), highlight the ability of influential families to take advantage of corrupt government officials and weak legal safeguards to appropriate wealth for themselves and their firms.

Along with the conditions of the institutional environment, the long-term macroeconomic context in the different countries of the region constitutes a further factor of heterogeneity that significantly influences

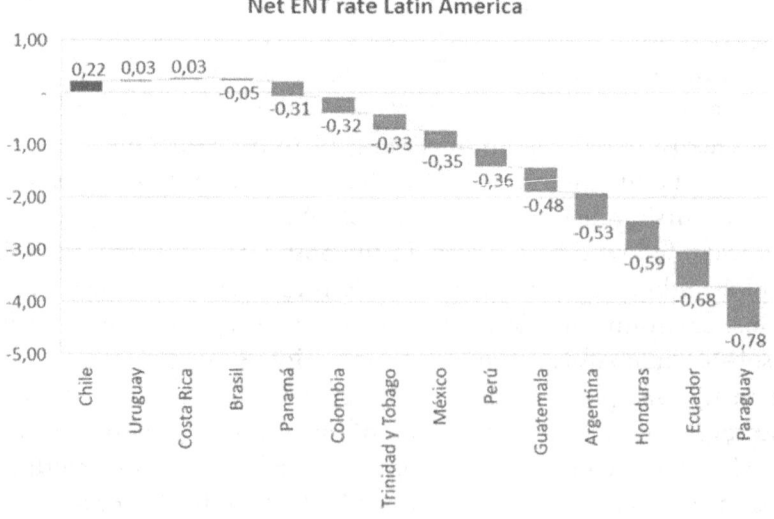

Fig. 5.1 Net entrepreneurship rate (*Source* Compiled by authors with data from World Bank, World Intellectual Property Organization and World Economic Forum, and Transparency International [2017–2019])

family businesses, which has fluctuated between cycles of expansion and stagnation. The latter is reflected in Argentina's agro-export stage at the end of the nineteenth century, mainly in the export of products such as meat, leather, and agro-food, which were conducted by local family businesses together with significant participation of foreign businesspeople, especially French and Belgian. As we have seen in Chapter 4 of this text, European migration supported the expansion of the economy, deepening the model of small family producers and groups of landowners while not yet establishing a predominant structure of large companies with significant weight for the local economy. As we will see in the following sections, diversified economic groups that emerged in the 1850s and progressed in the first third of the twentieth century became the elite of large companies in the region.

This context of institutional environment differences and long-term macroeconomic swings has shaped the strategies of Latin American family businesses in achieving their long-term sustainability goals, despite being less inclined to control outsiders compared to listed companies. Given their own complex structures, families may act more discreetly, as one business group may invest in political relationships, while another group business may benefit from this. Due to their opaque corporate governance features, family firms have greater political skills and greater capabilities in the pursuit of superior earnings (Morck & Yeung, 2004).

5.2 From State-Owned Companies to Large Family Groups

In emerging markets, governments are heavily involved in business decisions (Granovetter, 1995) and play an essential role for family-owned conglomerates. Kandemir et al. (2004) present the example of the Siam Cement Group in Thailand and the Salim and Astra companies in Indonesia, particularly in the expansion phase of the business. In Mexico, the commercial banking sector in the late 1800s underwent a process of "Mexicanization" when, with the help of state forces, foreign control was eliminated, and powerful family conglomerates or holding groups were established around domestic private banks.

Seen in perspective, Latin American countries have many features in common, such as specialization in natural or agricultural resources, heterogeneous productive structures with low productivity, and the persistence of a substantial informal sector in the context of weak state capacities. This has led to contrasting capitalist socioeconomic regimes, in some countries operating through reliance on markets to organize value creation and income distribution, and in others through the mediating role of socio-political commitments embedded in a series of institutional arrangements. Based on these criteria, four types of capitalism have been defined in Latin America: international outsourcing (Mexico), socio developmentalist (Brazil), rentier/liberal (Chile), and rentier/redistributive (Ecuador) (Bizberg, 2019).

Many of the weak states have been entrenched in rent-seeking behavior, with control exercised by elites who exploit their political and economic power for their benefit. Robinson and Acemoglu (2012) termed them "extractive institutions," meaning institutions designed to benefit elites.

The state's leading role in the region was strongly reflected in the application of intervention and import substitution industrialization policies. This period stretched from the end of the 1930s until after World War II in different nations of the region. These initiatives contributed to diversifying industrial capacity and meeting their consumer goods and part of the intermediate and capital goods with domestic production. These were followed by a process of investment and productive and technological transformation. In some countries, it was more intense than in others. Agriculture, especially in Argentina, Brazil, and Chile, benefited from applying technologies and production methods in the cultivation of land; many of the landowning families that were focused on basic agricultural production reaped the benefits of these innovations. On the other hand, the Central American countries, Ecuador, and Peru, lagged by not modernizing their agriculture and continuing with the primary export model. This differentiated the Southern Cone countries. Activities related to energy, communications, transportation, and other services achieved remarkable development and managed to develop a vigorous and early middle class with a large domestic market.

The next step was the build-up of concentration processes in family-owned companies that went on to constitute the first diversified business groups in Mexico, Argentina, Colombia, Chile, and Brazil. For the most part, these family-owned companies stemmed from the initial stages of development during the period of incorporation into the world market for agricultural and livestock products. Many of these families had been rooted since the end of the colonial period; many moved toward integration processes, alliances with other families, and permanent adaptation to changing and unstable cycles.

Family businesses in Argentina were concentrated in the manufacturing industry, in the production of parts and pieces for the automobile industry, and more innovative industrial sectors such as pharmaceuticals and chemicals. The case of family businesses in Mexico benefited from the post-1920 reforms, which fostered institutional conditions for entrepreneurial action, particularly in industry. Such incentives were oriented toward a protectionist economic nationalism. Business families linked to the oligarchy that supported the political system before the 1910 revolution were subjected to expropriation (Cerutti, 2000).

In the case of Colombia, the beginning of the twentieth century saw the rise of family businesses that rapidly formed the first economic groups. In the process, the activity of regional business families that came to control specific economic groups was of great relevance. It was during this period that the first companies of six of the economic groups were founded as family businesses (Rodríguez-Satizábal, 2010).

The impact of the application of policies based on import substitution—state interventionism—and its direct action in creating a publicly owned business sector reduced the capacity for entrepreneurship, damaging the prospects for private enterprise development. While industries such as the iron and steel industry and others that required significant capital, contributions were supervised by the state, in intermediate manufacturing industries, the opportunities of the restricted competitive environment were used to boost family businesses. This growth process continued with the expansion and diversification of new sectors that import substitution made possible, in some countries, even up to the 1970s. From then on, and stimulated by the states themselves, a completely new phase began. On the one hand, the poor management of state enterprises and the deficits in service supply prompted most Latin American countries to embark on privatization processes.

State-owned enterprises proved inefficient, produced low-quality goods and services, and generated more debt than profits. They became overstaffed as governments used them to generate and maintain employment. Shielded from the competition, state enterprises were often instructed to keep their prices below the level of cost recovery, leading to ever-increasing economic losses, in some cases reaching as much as 5 and 6% of GDP (Stan et al., 2014).

This privatization drive varied widely. Some countries with important state-owned sectors, such as Costa Rica, Ecuador, and Uruguay, privatized only a few companies. In contrast, others, such as Chile, Argentina, Bolivia, Panama, and Peru, sold state-owned companies for more than 10% of their GDP (Bruton et al., 2015). In Latin America, 75% of the revenues obtained from privatizations came from sales of utilities and infrastructure companies, 11% corresponded to the financial sector, and the remainder to the area of oil, gas, and manufacturing. Most countries have privatized their telecommunications, electricity, gas, and, to a lesser extent, water and sanitation services. However, the sale of state-owned railways, airlines, airports, and highways has not been as significant. In the financial and industrial sectors, privatizations were not so substantial because private participation was already widespread. Besides, most countries kept at least one official bank and retained control of companies linked to natural resources such as oil, gas, and copper. Even Chile decided not to privatize companies in critical sectors, such as copper, oil, banking, mail, railroads, and ports. A peculiar case is Argentina, which did not keep any major company in state ownership, except for some national and provincial banks and some local health companies. By contrast, Uruguay, which is comparable to Argentina in other respects, made the least progress in the privatization process in the entire region.

State-owned companies now in private hands significantly increased profitability and efficiency, with companies registering a 14% increase in net income ratio to sales. The most significant increases occurred in Peru and Argentina, where they amounted to approximately 20%. The main cause of this improvement in profitability has been a leap in efficiency. In fact, the privatizations led to a real plunge in unit costs. As for the sales per employee indicator, the results are also impressive: in Chile and Mexico, to cite the two most prominent cases, the ratio of sales per employee doubled in the privatized companies. In some specific companies, the increases were even higher. It may seem that success consisted of continuing to do the same thing with lower costs and less personnel, but this is not the case. One of the most striking findings is that the companies' output increased considerably as a result of the privatizations. The largest increases were recorded in Mexico and Colombia, where average production increased 68 and 59%, respectively.

We can see that in this short period up to the mid-1850s, family businesses went from being mere producers of semi-finished agricultural goods and, in very exceptional cases, exporters of other raw materials to be located in intermediate production sectors as a result of import substitution policies. The first diversified economic groups were established at this point until the new impulse given by the purchase of state-owned companies—privatization processes,—which, depending on the country, became relevant at the end of the 1960s and onwards.

5.3 Family Business Group Diversity

From a general perspective, the literature defines the business group (Morck & Yeung, 2003) as a plurality of companies, most of which are autonomous, but at the same time, have a leading company that is in control of all the companies that make up the aggregation itself. The parent company is presented as an organization that owns most shares of one or more operating companies—under its shareholding control—and carries out overseeing and coordinating these companies' activities. Similarly, Khanna and Rivkin (2001) indicate that business groups are clusters consisting of several legally independent firms united by formal and informal ties and subjected to coordinated action.

Research on business groups in emerging markets has proliferated as developing countries have grown in economic importance (Khanna &

Palepu, 1997). Furthermore, while they are legally independent entities, they often "take coordinated action" (Khanna & Rivkin, 2001), leading to negative externalities in the markets they operate. Another study indicates that the proportion of group-affiliated firms is substantial in some areas of the Asia Pacific, with prevalence levels ranging from 25% of listed firms in the Philippines to 65% in Indonesia (Carney & Gedajlovic, 2002).

Considering the different morphologies that a business group can take, we present the various forms that family business groups adopt.

The first distinction is based on the connections between their parent companies. Therefore, they can be divided into hierarchical or hegemonic groups, both characterized by a vertical structure, whereby a hierarchy is established between the legally distinct units by means of the control relations the family exerts.

A field of study has been to investigate the motivations underlying the formation of such aggregations, most often of an economic nature, namely, related to the maintenance, improvement, or return of long-term economic equilibrium conditions for the companies involved. Non-economic objectives have also been investigated, such as increasing credit capital, exploiting stock leverage or financial leverage, facilitating family business operations and generational succession, IPOs of only specific activities, reducing the tax burden, and creating production units. It has even been tested for pursuing other hidden or illicit objectives (Yiu et al., 2007), such as the recent case[2] of the controlling family of the Odebrecht company in Brazil (Zysman-Quirós, 2019).

Considering the economic-productive relationship existing between companies, it is common to classify business groups into horizontal integration, which arises from the development of companies that operate in the same economic sector. They carry out similar production processes and produce or distribute similar products and services. One example of this type of economic group is Manuelita[3] in Colombia, owned and operated by the fourth generation of the Eder family; it is one of the largest agro-industrial companies in the Cauca region of eastern

---

[2] https://www.economist.com/business/2015/08/20/principles-and-values.

[3] https://www.manuelita.com/plataformas-de-negocios/.

Colombia. Apart from the advantages of scale, the emergence of such groups is stimulated by the advantages of supplies and the ambition to achieve more solid sales positions that allow them to exert a certain influence on their markets and, in part, to reduce competition.

Another type of business organization is the so-called vertical, made up of companies which, despite operating in the same or related sectors, carry out successive stages of the production process, as in the case of the Gerdau Group[4] of Brazil, one of the most important companies in steel production, founded and controlled by the Gerdau Johannpeter family.

The conglomerate, in which the individual units that make up the group operate in different and distant sectors and may have some minimal productive interrelationships, is the most diversified manner of grouping companies under a single owner. An example from Peru is the case of the Romero Group[5] with multiple businesses in the areas of food, manufacturing, logistics, infrastructure, and commerce. Risk diversification is the main advantage of conglomerate-type groups.

These patterns of the typical group of multinational companies are becoming more and more widespread in the less complex family business environment in Latin America, as they have been adapted to the family needs, allowing tax planning in the succession processes. As a matter of fact, Latin American business families have relied more on the rather legal development of the spin-off of companies, constituting the figure of family holdings. Choosing the different legal figures has different objectives, such as giving continuity to the family business, designing a profitable return for the family members, facilitating the transfer of ownership to the next generation, and even obtaining tax advantages. According to the legislation of each country, the most common configuration that family businesses can adopt in Latin America is two primary forms: the shareholding company, open or closed, composed by holding shares whether they are traded on the stock exchange, and the limited liability company, which can be limited in which the owners are accountable up to the value of their contributions.

---

[4] https://www2.gerdau.com.br/quem-somos/governanca-corporativa.
[5] http://www.gruporomero.com.pe/es-PE/empresas/.

5.4   Latin American Multinational Family Business

Latin America is characterized by a strong presence of family businesses and extremely resilient entrepreneurs, given the adverse conditions of institutional quality. To compete with the best global players and corporations, many family businesses in the region have set out to professionalize their processes and hire talent from outside the family and compete in global markets. These decisions have been not exempted from ambition, optimism and patience, and a long-term view.

The moment at which a family business decides to internationalize depends on several factors. This process is slower compared to non-family businesses, but the degree reached is almost the same in the long run. The explanation is simple and practice, family owners are likely to be reluctant to create relationships in foreign networks and require higher levels of knowledge before opening to international markets (Pukall & Calabrò, 2014).

Falabella,[6] the largest retailer in Latin America with revenues of US$14.6 billion (2017), is an example of this. It began in 1889 when the Italian immigrant, Salvatore Falabella, opened the first large tailor shop in Chile. The business grew hand in hand, with his son Arnaldo and then Alberto Solari—Arnaldo's son-in-law. Solari was the one who incorporated new product lines and transformed the family business into department stores. Later, in 1980, Reinaldo Solari took over the group's management together with his nephew, Juan Cúneo Solari. Both built other business lines, such as the financial business, and promoted international expansion in Peru, Argentina, Brazil, and Colombia. Only in the fourth generation of the family was this process consolidated.

As in the previous case, the overseas expansion of many family-owned companies tends to implement strategies that focus on their core business rather than attempting the arduous path of diversification. Collaboration with the right local partners and reputation are success factors in this type of process. Emerging markets offer great business opportunities for family-owned companies.

---

[6] https://investors.falabella.com/English/about-us/default.aspx#section=history.

As we have already indicated above, the socio-economic development of Latin America can be divided into two major historical periods: the first one from the colonial period up to independence from the Crowns of Spain and Portugal and then the establishment of the first independence republics up to the present day. This last period was born the major and endurance family firms, only just over 200 years, well below the history of family businesses in Asia and Europe. Their internationalization processes have been going on for more than 500 years.

Since mid-century, Latin American family businesses have expanded globally and have become Global Latinas (Casanova, 2009). As a result, Latin American investment in developed and emerging markets has increased considerably. While natural resources still account for most Latin American exports, the remainder is made up of a wide variety of products and services ranging from information technology products and services to steel, electricity, wine, cosmetics, and increasingly services.

According to the América Economía[7] report on the 500 largest Latin American companies published in 2019, Brazil leads the ranking with 211 companies. Mexico stands with 120, Chile with 72, Peru with 32, Colombia with 30, and Argentina with 23. Most of these companies are Latin American family-owned.

Some examples are Vale mining company—Vecchiola family—and the company JBS/Friboi—Batista family—both Brazilian, which are among the top ten in Latin America. América Móvil of Mexico—Slim Family—whose case we will review in detail at the end of this chapter, constitute examples of multinational family businesses. In fact, Forbes ranking places seven billionaires in the world's 100 are from Latin American: two in Brazil, two in Mexico, two in Colombia, and one in Chile.

The expansion of successful Latin American multinational starts with their home market. Companies from emerging countries try to avoid mistakes in their international development since their debt capacity and financial resources are usually smaller. Within home markets, information flows better, and thus the competitive landscape, customers, and

---

[7] https://www.americaeconomia.com/negocios-industrias/estas-son-las-500-empresas-mas-gra ndes-de-latinoamerica-2019.

suppliers are better known, and talent is easier to attract. Networks and ties between countries in a home market are closer than outside it.

The following are some examples of multinational family businesses in the context of some representative countries.

In Mexico, the institutional change with the Code of Commerce of 1889 stimulated the birth of large companies and created a regime with oligarchic biases and defined new rules of the game in economic matters. This encouraged foreign investment and connected the territory with more than 20,000 km of railroads, integrating Mexico's north-central region with the United States' economy in the midst of the industrial revolution. Regional dynamics, and the consequent emergence of business families closely connected to political power, were nourished by both markets. Monterrey, located in the northeast, was the most defined and pioneering. A number of these groups survive to this day. Some of these families owning the strongest business groups are the Slim family, the Carso group, and the second generation. Zambrano family, owners of the Cemex group in its fourth generation. Garza Sada Lagüera and Garza Sada Sada groups, owners of FEMSA and Alfa. Servitje family, owners of Grupo Bimbo in the third generation, and Bringas family, owners of Soriana in the second generation.

The Brazilian case is somewhat different from the Mexican case. Brazil did not have such open processes of business promotion. Although many family businesses contributed significantly to the development and industrialization of the Brazilian economy, many companies did not stand the test of time, and an important part of the history of family businesses in Brazil is missing. The ranking[8] carried out by St. Gallen University presents twelve multinational family businesses that have lasted until today. Among which stand out for their size, the Moreira Salles family and the Souza Aranha family, owners of Banco Itaú with revenues of 28 billion and 100,000 employees, and the case of Organizações Globo owned 100% by the Marinho family, which controls the main mass media enterprises, such as television, radio, and publishing.

As indicated above, Argentina's family business conglomerates evolved from the globalization stage of its economy between 1870 and 1914.

---

[8] https://familybusinessindex.com/.

During this period, the country experienced an accelerated expansion based on its integration into the world market as an exporter of raw materials and food. It then went through a process of import substitution, in which deliberate industrial policies were implemented, accentuating protectionism, and promoting the creation of state-owned companies in strategic sectors. Local companies that survived directed their efforts to the domestic market. Consequently, the share of Argentine companies among the 100 most prominent in the region declined, while the share of foreign firms increased.

Unlike in any other country, Argentina has such a high proportion of large family businesses founded by migrants. Some have survived until today—Menéndez and Braun families with La Anónima, a retail chain. Others that did not survive, closed, merged, or were sold to foreign groups, such as Quilmes, Astra, and Alpargatas, and other moderately internationalized food companies such as Bagley and Terrabusi.

Some of the outstanding cases that survive are those of the Rocca Family that founded Techint, largely due to the strength of the Italian-Argentine business community. Another case is the Molinos Río de la Plata company of the Pérez Companc family and the Braun family of Banco Galicia.

In Colombia, the case of multinational family businesses is relatively more recent than in other countries. For one thing, a zeal and veto of public information on who are the businessmen and families behind the large companies exist due to the practice of kidnapping for ransom.[9] But above all, it is only in the last 50 years that the family economic groups have advanced in the internationalization process and started to enter the group of the Multilatinas. In 1975, nine of the 24 largest non-financial conglomerates were family-owned (Pombo, & Gutiérrez, 2011). Family groups that have achieved internationalization are Sarmiento Angulo, Santo Domingo, and Ardila Lulle.

Furthermore, the case of Peru, along with Mexico and Chile, has inherited a long history of development of family businesses that have internationalized as economic groups. This begins at the end of the nineteenth century when the Peruvian economy recovered from the

---

[9] https://www.economist.com/the-americas/2012/03/03/deliverance.

War of the Pacific (1879–1883). The recovery was linked both to the political stability and to a new export boom based on the diversification of commodities—minerals, sugar, cotton, rubber, and oil—primary industry with a predominance of foreign direct investment. These economic policies favored free foreign trade and the consolidation of large family businesses.

Given this solid internal development, 23% of the business families from the early 1900s to 1960 were of foreign origin, primarily European (Portocarrero, 1992). Although sole proprietorships predominated, partnerships between families were unusual. Another frequent practice was vertical integration, for example, the Aspilliga Anderson Company, owners of the Cayaltí and Palto Agricultural Business. The brothers invested the surplus from their sugar exports in the financial local industry: Banco Italiano, Banco Popular and Banco Internacional, and the insurance companies Internacional and Rímac, and in the real estate sector in the city of Lima (Portocarrero, 2006).

In the years between 1968 and 1990, the political and economic history of Peru was particularly complicated. The country went from a military dictatorship, which transformed the forms of property and state intervention in the economy, to a fragile democracy that had to face a world economic crisis, a hyperinflationary process, and the threat of the subversive group Sendero Luminoso (Thorp, 1984). During these complicated years, entrepreneurial families that were considered of the second rank in the previous period assumed a leading role, as it was the case of the Brescia and Romero families.

In the 1989 ranking of the 500 most important companies in Peru, there were 346 family-owned firms and 47 state-owned firms (Rojas, 1994). Another striking fact is the reduced longevity of Peruvian family businesses. The few companies that are over one hundred years old, and are still owned by Peruvian businessmen, are the Lindley Corporation and Tejidos San Jacinto—Isola family—and the Ibérica company— Vidaurrázaga family. The Romero family is the one that has managed to remain active for four generations in the business world and has been successful in its internationalization processes. One of the oldest family companies is the Gloria Group.[10] Throughout its 70 years of existence, it was first a transnational company with minority participation of Peruvian capitals and then became a family company after its purchase by the Rodriguez brothers in 1986. Backus and Johnston, which was bought by a foreign company, has followed the opposite path.

Another country with a long tradition of family businesses and successful cases of internationalization is Chile. In general terms, it has experienced significant economic growth, stimulated by its insertion into the world economy as an exporter of raw materials. This process enabled the emergence of new family-owned businesses that differed from the traditional ones based on trade and land tenure associated with the colonial era. This new group of families carried out a modernization characterized by the rise of different industrial, mining, and agricultural initiatives.

However, most of the great business families of the nineteenth century did not survive the passage of time. Therefore, most of today's business families are relatively young and are in the second or third generation and very few in the fourth generation.

The first three family groups are the Luksic, Angelini, and Matte families, which own companies in unrelated sectors, while other families are more focused on an industrial sector. This is the case of the Paulmann families—owners of the Cencosud Group with presence in Peru, Colombia, and Argentina—and the Solari, Cúneo, and del Río families—owners of the Falabella Group. Another family that has been successful in internationalization processes is the Cueto and Von Appen families in airlines and maritime transportation, respectively.

In the following section, we will present two cases of companies that have internationalized their operations.

---

[10] https://www.grupogloria.com/gloriaHISTORIA.html.

5.5   Case Studies

5.5.1   Carvajal Group—Colombia

Grupo Carvajal is one of the best-known multinational companies in Colombia and is still in the hands of the founding family. The company has operations in more than 15 countries in Latin America, Spain, and the United States, in the publishing, printing, paper, school, and office products, packaging, and other sectors. Since its foundation, the company has diversified into furniture, process outsourcing, information management, environmental music, and business services.

The origins of Grupo Carvajal date back to 1869 after Manuel Carvajal and some friends bought an old printing press that was used to publish a weekly newspaper called La Opinión. Through the newspaper pages, they spread the political ideas of the Conservative Party of Colombia, which at that time was engaged in a struggle with the liberals. Although these initial motivations would never have been projected to what it is today, with operating profits over 100 million dollars as of 2018.[11]

Several years after this foray into politics, the company became Carvajal, S.A., announcing its operations in the city of Cali in 1904, and together with his two eldest sons—Alberto and Hernando—expanded rapidly. Unfortunately, the joint work of the first and second generation was cut short with the founder's death in 1912. However, his children continued to manage the business, expanding into the sale of paper products and other office supplies.

During the 1920s, the emergence of new industries in Colombia prompted Carvajal to venture into multiple businesses, diversifying into the construction area, the marketing of automobiles and trucks, being representatives of General Motors in Colombia. They also imported and distributed adding and calculating machines, safes, electric lamps, and clocks, among other items. Within their business vision, and despite being amid the Great Economic Depression of 1929, they purchased a

---

[11] Annual report, 2018: https://www.carvajal.com/wp-content/uploads/2019/04/Informe-Anual-Carvajal-2018.pdf.

very advanced machine for its time for lithographic printing in Germany and dedicated themselves to the nascent offset printing industry. Unfortunately, during this period, Hernando Carvajal Borrero suffered a brain hemorrhage. So, he could not carry out any planned succession process, so his eldest son, Manuel Carvajal Sinisterra, assumed the presidency at the age of 23 and was its president for the next 32 years, until his death at the age of 55. During these years, he led the company and positioned it as the leading printer and publisher in Latin America.

As we have seen in this section, many governments carried out the import substitution model for long periods. As a result, Carvajal benefited from state protection.

Throughout this period, the company expanded across Colombia, in addition to making investments abroad. This entrepreneurial drive allowed them in the 1950s to establish new business units such as personalized stationery and publish the first yellow pages along with launching the first international operations in Puerto Rico.

One of Carvajal's most internationalized companies is Grupo Editorial Norma, which merged with Bico Internacional due to a restructuring in 2009, even though Norma had existed since 1960. They take advantage of the marketing and logistics synergies that can be shared between the publishing business and the stationery and supplies business.

Grupo Editorial Norma is dedicated to creating, designing, producing, and marketing books for education and entertainment in all genres and formats for all kinds of audiences. In addition to its divisions Norma Educación and Norma Libros, this group includes the publishing imprints Kapelusz Editora, Editorial Farben, Parramón Ediciones, Granica, and Belacqva.

In recent years, the publishing industry has been affected by a decline in demand for books and the increased competitive intensity of Spanish companies. However, it has focused its efforts on improving working capital by optimizing its inventories, rationalizing the number of titles launched in the market, and increasing its geographic focus. This has involved reducing operations in countries such as El Salvador, Panama, and the Dominican Republic. As a result, Grupo Editorial Norma currently has operations in Argentina, Chile, Brazil, Peru,

Ecuador, Colombia, Spain, Venezuela, Panama, Costa Rica, El Salvador, Guatemala, Mexico, Puerto Rico, and the Dominican Republic.

At the core of Carvajal's long-term success are its vision and a set of values that emphasize both profitability and community focus. The company's vision statement is "to become a leading Latin American multinational and a preferred supplier of products and services, maintaining the highest standards of excellence and quality." The above reflects the culture of four generations in command and the family's commitment to enhance the social value and well-being of the communities in which they operate.

Carvajal, S.A., is currently a multinational company that operates in six business areas: Carvajal Education, Carvajal Packaging, Carvajal Spaces, Carvajal Pulp and Paper, Carvajal Communication Solutions, and Carvajal Technology and Services.

To honor one of the patriarchs, Manuel Carvajal Sinisterra, the family transferred 40% of the shares to the Hernando Carvajal Borrero Foundation in 1961, which was renamed Carvajal Foundation in 1977 and has been the company's largest shareholder ever since. The foundation dedicates a large part of its efforts to improving living conditions in impoverished areas of Cali.

5.5.2 Carso Group—Mexico

As already mentioned in this section, family-owned companies that diversify their businesses, especially those that have migrated their business and ownership structure as multilatinas, often adopt a conglomerate structure.

Grupo Carso is owned by the Slim family and comprises hotels, mines, railroads, shopping centers, among others. The different branches of this conglomerate have helped it in times of crisis to offset losses in one sector against the others.

The company was founded in Mexico in 1980 and was initially known as Grupo Galas. Between 1980 and 1989, the company acquired the majority of the shares of Cigatam, Artes Gráficas Unidas, Fábricas de Papel Loreto y Peña Pobre, Galas de México, Sanborns, Empresas Frisco,

Industrias Nacobre, and Porcelanite Holding. In 1990, the company changed its name to Grupo Carso, and in June, a placement of the issuer's shares was carried out in the Mexican Stock Exchange. That same year, Carso, together with Southwestern Bell International Holding Corp., France Cables Et Radio, and a group of investors, took control over Telmex through a public bidding process. This acquisition was undoubtedly the first step toward becoming a multinational company.

In one interview,[12] Carlos Slim commented:

From the beginning I was involved in many businesses. I bought a bottling company. I started an investment firm, a construction company, a real estate business, and I started five or six different work areas. And I think, and I understand that there is a lot of confusion between the businessman, the entrepreneur, the executives and the investors. There are three different people. But in small businesses, typically, the same person does all three. He or she is the investor, the businessman, the entrepreneur and the executive, the CEO. So, it was very clear to me that being a CEO and a businessman were wholly different and that being an investor is also different. And the further I pursued my career I started working with executives. My job as a businessman was to work with the executives and the CEOs to develop those capabilities.

From 1991 to 1995, Carso acquired shares in companies from very different industrial sectors, Compañía Euzkadi, Grupo Condumex, Grupo Aluminio, and General Tire de México and 80% of the capital of Sears México. It also owns a 49.9% stake in Philip Morris Mexico.

In 1999, Grupo Sanborns redefined its corporate structure as the commercial unit of Grupo Carso and purchased Pastelería El Globo, which was sold to Grupo Bimbo sometime later. Carso also acquired the capital stock of Ferrosur, the holding company of the operating rights of the Mexico-Veracruz railroad. During 2003, Grupo Sanborns acquired 6 JC Penney stores and 13 stores of Pastelerías Monterrey. Grupo Condumex ventured into the oil platform construction business. In 2004 Sanborns acquired all of the shares of Dorian's Tijuana and opened three stores in El Salvador. In 2005 Carso Infraestructura y Construcción carried out a public offering through the Mexican Stock

---

[12] Interview with Larry King, 2013 Global Conference Milken Institute.

Exchange. In 2007, the automotive ring and sleeves manufacturing business in Condumex was sold, stakes in the tobacco business were reduced, and Porcelanite was sold. The first Saks Fifth Avenue store is opened.

In 2010 Grupo Carso sold the mining and real estate business of Minera Frisco and Inmuebles Carso. In 2013 Grupo Sanborns placed a public offering of shares in Mexico and abroad. Carso then sold the remainder of its stake in Philip Morris Mexico.

We can see in this brief account the profile of Carlos Slim as a serial entrepreneur through Grupo Carso, one of the largest and most important conglomerates in Latin America.

The Group's companies generate 217 thousand direct jobs and more than 500 thousand indirect jobs in Mexico. Its main subsidiaries are Grupo Sanborns, formed by a chain of 172 stores, Grupo Condumex, an industrial subsidiary of Grupo Carso, which concentrates on the manufacture and marketing of products and services for the construction and infrastructure, energy, automobile, telecommunications, and mining markets. América Móvil operates in 18 countries with a total of 269 thousand mobile telephone service subscribers, also Slim´s diversification covers the main shareholder of The New York Times, controlling 16.8% of the company's stock, among others.

5.6   Chapter Summary

As we have mentioned in this section, the business group is defined as a plurality of companies, most of which may be autonomous and unrelated—such as the Carso group. But, at the same time, it has one leading company that exercises control over all the companies that make up the aggregation itself. In contrast, other groups are more integrated within their industrial sector, such as the Carvajal Group in Colombia.

This way of organizing companies has also been criticized because it could put institutions at risk by operating outside regulations, leading to negative externalities in the markets in which they operate (Khanna & Rivkin, 2001). Alternatively, they may be designed with non-economic objectives such as increasing credit capital, exploiting financial leverage, or even other hidden or illicit objectives (Yiu et al., 2007).

A further feature of family groups and large family conglomerates in Latin America is related to their ability to adapt to institutional conditions. In fact, adverse effects of the institutional conditions experienced by family firms in emerging economies such as Latin American countries have been suggested. A related aspect is that family firms in the region have a greater capacity to fill institutional vacuums. In this type of scenario, family networks help in market development through cooperation among small firms. But, on the other hand, they highlight the ability of influential families to take advantage of corrupt government officials.

However, we also observed substantial heterogeneity gaps in the number of multilatinas companies and the number of economic groups in the region's countries. This situation is not necessarily correlated with the size of their economy as measured by GDP. As in the case of Mexico and Brazil (USD 1.3 trillion and USD 1.8 trillion, respectively), where Mexico has a large number of multinational companies concentrated in a few economic groups. In Brazil, on the other hand, there is an inverse effect, with many economic groups, but very few of them are internationalized.

This section has also shown that family businesses in the region are somewhat reluctant to internationalization processes compared to non-family businesses. Nevertheless, in the long run, the degree achieved is roughly the same. The explanation is simple: family owners need to build relationships in foreign networks and require higher levels of knowledge before opening up to international markets, this is in line with Pukall and Calabrò (2014).

References

Baumol, W. J. (1990). Entrepreneurship: Productive, unproductive and destructive. *Journal of Political Economy, 98*(5), 893–921.

Benavente, J. M., Crespi, G., Katz, J., & Stumpo, G. (1997). New problems and opportunities for industrial development in Latin America. *Oxford Development Studies, 25*(3), 261–277.

Bizberg, I. (2019). *Diversity of capitalisms in Latin America* (Vol. 49). Palgrave Macmillan.

Bruton, G. D., Peng, M. W., Ahlstrom, D., Stan, C., & Xu, K. (2015). State-owned enterprises around the world as hybrid organizations. *Academy of Management Perspectives, 29*(1), 92–114.

Camargo, M. I. B. (2021). Institutions, institutional quality, and international competitiveness: Review and examination of future research directions. *Journal of Business Research, 128*, 423–435.

Carney, M., & Gedajlovic, E. (2002). The co-evolution of institutional environments and organizational strategies: The rise of family business groups in the ASEAN region. *Organization Studies, 23*(1), 1–29.

Carney, M., Van Essen, M., Estrin, S., & Shapiro, D. (2018). Business groups reconsidered: Beyond paragons and parasites. *Academy of Management Perspectives, 32*(4), 493–516.

Casanova, L. (2009). *Global latinas: Latin America's emerging multinationals.* Springer.

Cerutti, M. (2000). Propietarios, empresarios y empresa en el norte de México: Monterrey: de 1848 a la glabalización. Siglo XXI.

Gedajlovic, E., Carney, M., Chrisman, J. J., & Kellermanns, F. W. (2012). The adolescence of family firm research: Taking stock and planning for the future. *Journal of Management, 38*(4), 1010–1037.

Granovetter, M. (1995). Coase revisited: Business groups in the modern economy. *Industrial and Corporate Change, 4*(1), 93–130.

Greif, A. (1994). On the political foundations of the late medieval commercial revolution: Genoa during the twelfth and thirteenth centuries. *The Journal of Economic History, 54*(2), 271–287.

Kim, D., Kandemir, D., & Cavusgil, S. T. (2004). The role of family conglomerates in emerging markets: What western companies should know. *Thunderbird International Business Review, 46*(1), 13–38.

Khanna, T., & Palepu, K. (1997). Why focused strategies. *Harvard Business Review, 75*(4), 41–51.

Khanna, T., & Rivkin, J. W. (2001). Estimating the performance effects of business groups in emerging markets. *Strategic Management Journal, 22*(1), 45–74.

Morck, R., & Yeung, B. (2003). Agency problems in large family business groups. *Entrepreneurship Theory and Practice, 27*(4), 367–382.

Morck, R., & Yeung, B. (2004). Family control and the rent–seeking society. *Entrepreneurship Theory and Practice, 28*(4), 391–409.

North, D. (1999). Chapter 3: Institutions and economic growth: A historical introduction. In *International Political Economy*, Taylor & Francis Ltd/Books.

North, D. C. (2002). *Institutions and economic growth: A historical introduction*, (pp. 57–69). Routledge.

Pombo, C., & Gutiérrez, L. H. (2011). Outside directors, board interlocks and firm performance: Empirical evidence from Colombian business groups. *Journal of Economics and Business, 63*(4), 251–277.

Portocarrero, G. (1992). Del racismo al mestizaje: una apuesta por la integración. *Los quinientos años: un espacio para la reflexión*, 31–41.

Portocarrero, F. (2006). *Wealth and philanthropy: The economic elite in Peru, 1916–1960*. (Doctoral dissertation, University of Oxford).

Pukall, T. J., & Calabro, A. (2014). The internationalization of family firms: A critical review and integrative model. *Family Business Review, 27*(2), 103–125.

Rautiainen, M., Rosa, P., Pihkala, T., Parada, M. J., & Cruz, A. D. (2019). *The family business group phenomenon*. Springer International Publishing.

Robinson, J. A., & Acemoglu, D. (2012). *Why nations fail: The origins of power, prosperity and poverty*. London: Profile.

Rodríguez-Satizábal, B. (2010). *Beyond the large business enterprise: The rise of business groups in Colombia, 1974–1998*. MSc (Economic History) Dissertation. London School of Economics and Political Science.

Rojas, J. (1994). La reforma del sistema financiero peruano, 1990–1995. *Economía, 17*(33–34), 149–198.

Scott, W. R. (1995). *Institutions and organizations*. Thousand oaks, CA: Sage Publications.

Sobel, R. S. (2008). Testing Baumol: Institutional quality and the productivity of entrepreneurship. *Journal of Business Venturing, 23*(6), 641–655.

Stan, C. V., Peng, M. W., & Bruton, G. D. (2014). Slack and the performance of state-owned enterprises. *Asia Pacific Journal of Management, 31*(2), 473–495.

Stosberg, J. (2018). *Political risk and the institutional environment for foreign direct investment in Latin America: An empirical analysis with a case study on Mexico* (p. 342). Peter Lang International Academic Publishers.

Thorp, R. (1984). Políticas de ajuste en el Perú, 1978–1985: Los efectos de una crisis prolongada. *Economia, 7*(14), 81–115.

Weingast, B. R. (1993). Constitutions as governance structures: The political foundations of secure markets. *Journal of Institutional and Theoretical Economics (JITE)*, 286–311.

Yiu, D. W., Lu, Y., Bruton, G. D., & Hoskisson, R. E. (2007). Business groups: An integrated model to focus future research. *Journal of Management Studies, 44*(8), 1551–1579.

Zysman-Quirós, D. (2019). White-Collar crime in South and Central America: Corporate-State crime, governance, and the high impact of the Odebrecht corruption case. *The Handbook of White-Collar Crime,* 363–380.

6

The New Wave of Global Family Entrepreneurs (the Fourth Wave)

This chapter describes the new wave of modern family businesses created by family entrepreneurs who have known to globalize their business through information technologies, social networks, and megatrends since the 2000s to the present in Latin America. Likewise, we describe the meaning of family entrepreneurship, its triggers in Latin America, and the challenges of entrepreneurial families. This chapter also describes two exemplary cases of global family entrepreneurs from Chile (Fernando Fischmann, founder of Crystal Lagoons) and Mexico (Rene Freudenberg, owner of Interlub Group).

This section provides the reader the following learning objectives:

- To detect the triggers of the success of a global family entrepreneurship as a new form of wealth creation in Latin America.
- To analyze two successful cases of continuity of Latin American family businesses that survive until today and that are the product of this period.

© The Author(s), under exclusive license to Springer Nature
Switzerland AG 2021
C. G. Müller and F. Sandoval-Arzaga, *Family Business Heterogeneity
in Latin America*, Palgrave Studies in Family Business Heterogeneity,
https://doi.org/10.1007/978-3-030-78931-2_6

6.1   Family Entrepreneurship: The Key to Generational Continuity

Family entrepreneurship is key to the continuity of business families. Generating new businesses and innovating business models ensures that family ownership is maintained across generations, as the environment is changing and it is necessary for today's business families to be dynamic and open to economic, social and technological transformations.

This notion implies making a paradigm shift in the business family, that is, to stop being a *family business* in which the family lives off a single business and, instead, become an *entrepreneurial family* in which the family is continuously innovating its business model and generating new businesses.

Thus, family entrepreneurship should not only be understood at the level of the business, but also at the level of the family, which promotes and encourages entrepreneurship as part of its own continuity through the generations. Therefore, family entrepreneurship implies to be part of the social capital and the legacy of a business family, as well as preparing the new generations as entrepreneurs, promoting entrepreneurial family leadership, and consolidating families as entrepreneurs (Allen & Gartner, 2021).

To become an entrepreneurial family, one must combine the entrepreneurial orientation of the business with the unique capabilities of the business family to create financial and social value across generations. This is called transgenerational entrepreneurship (Habbershon et al., 2010).

The entrepreneurial orientation of the company is that which allows it to create innovations in the product-market binomial and to take the risk of creating new businesses. Entrepreneurial orientation can be measured through 5 dimensions: autonomy, innovation, risk-taking, proactivity and competitive aggressiveness (Lumpkin & Dess, 1996; Miller, 1983).

Autonomy means that there is freedom within the organization to be generating new ideas. Innovation is the company's ability to convert those ideas into new products or services, new business models, or process improvements. Risk-taking is measured by the amount of resources committed to creating innovations. Proactivity is the company's ability to take advantage of the opportunities offered by the market. And finally, competitive aggressiveness is the actions the firm takes to beat the competition.

In family businesses, entrepreneurial orientation can be enhanced if combined with *familiness*, that is, the unique set of resources and capabilities that a family business has that gives it a competitive advantage (Habbershon & Williams, 1999). These resources are financial, human, social, cultural, and knowledge capital (Habbershon et al., 2010). These resources refer, for example, to the positive impact of the business family's leadership, its network of contacts, the use of financial resources, the culture and values that the family imbues the business with, its decision-making and governance mechanisms, and its ability to share and transfer tacit knowledge between generations.

If a business family uses familiness to drive the entrepreneurial orientation of the company and does so by combining the wisdom of previous generations with the dynamics of the new generations then it becomes an entrepreneurial family.

According to the 2019 Global Family Business Survey, conducted by the STEP Project,[1] Latin American Family Businesses show a higher entrepreneurial orientation than the global average and are above family businesses in North America and Europe. It should be noted that they are at a higher level in autonomy, risk-taking, and competitive aggressiveness; however, they have a lower level of innovation.

From the same STEP survey but from the Latin American report called "The Succession Process in Family Businesses in Latin America",[2] the survey included 407 family businesses in Mexico, Brazil, Colombia, Venezuela, Chile, Ecuador, Peru, and Guatemala. The survey included 407 family businesses in Mexico, Brazil, Colombia, Venezuela, Chile,

---

[1] The STEP Project has 48 affiliated universities from around the world. The survey included more than 1800 family businesses from 5 regions of the world (Europe, North America, Latin America, Asia and Middle East and Africa). The report was prepared by A. Calabro (IPAG Business School) and A. Valentino (ESCE International Business School).

[2] The Latin American STEP Project includes 10 affiliated universities from different countries. The report was prepared by Y. Rodriguez (ICESI, Colombia), P. Monteferrante (IESA, Venezuela), L. Diaz-Matajira (UNIANDES, Colombia), and F. Sandoval-Arzaga (Tecnológico de Monterrey, Mexico).

Ecuador, Peru, and Guatemala. In terms of Latin America as a whole in its entrepreneurial orientation this report tells us the following:

- Competitive aggressiveness
  - 47% of managers initiate actions to which competitors respond.
  - 51% of managers tend to introduce or introduce new products and services when dealing with competitors.
- Risk-taking
  - 37% of management teams in Latin America favor low-risk projects.
  - 33% take a cautious "wait and see" approach rather than a bolder, riskier approach.
- Innovation
  - 52% of Latin American business families have introduced new product or service lines in the last 5 years.
  - Only 28% have made major changes in this regard.

Although, as we have already said, the average Latin American entrepreneurial orientation is higher than in other regions of the world, these data show moderate aggressiveness and innovation, and cautious risk-taking. This means that the family entrepreneurship paradigm has yet to be developed in Latin America.

The following chart shows a comparison of Latin American countries in which some of the elements of entrepreneurial orientation are taken into account, ordered from highest to lowest level of entrepreneurial orientation by dimension (Table 6.1).

Latin American family businesses differ in their level of entrepreneurial orientation. Guatemala and Brazil stand out as the countries with the highest level in this aspect; Ecuador and Chile as the lowest; Mexico and Colombia with a consistent average position; and Venezuela and Peru with varying levels depending on size.

Business families capable of becoming entrepreneurial families consistently and systematically ensure their continuity and are part of the emergence of the new wave, the new generation of family businesses in Latin America.

Table 6.1 Comparison of Latin American countries

Aggressiveness—Initiates action before competitors	Risk-taking—Take on high-risk projects	Innovation—New products in last 5 years
Guatemala	Guatemala	Brazil
Venezuela	Brazil	Peru
Brazil	Colombia	Guatemala
Mexico	Venezuela	Mexico
Colombia	Mexico	Colombia
Ecuador	Chile	Chile
Peru Chile	Peru Ecuador	Ecuador
		Venezuela

Source Latin American STEP Report 2019: "The succession process in Latin American family businesses"

6.2 The Takeoff of Family Entrepreneurship in Latin America

The emergence of family entrepreneurship in Latin America has to do with three basic components: social and technological megatrends, the emergence of a new generation of entrepreneurs, and the capacity of business families to promote entrepreneurship in the new generations.

6.2.1 Social and Technological Megatrends

The analysis of megatrends is important in two ways. On the one hand, it helps us to understand how the accelerated changes of the second half of the twentieth century to date have modified the way human groups and companies act, and, on the other hand, as a way of looking to the future and generating undertakings that will satisfy this future society: The environment modifies us at the same time as we modify it.

Megatrends are major social and technological changes that affect the world in a time period of ten to fifteen years (Naisbitt & Aburdene, 1990) and have a major effect on society. The ability to identify business opportunities based on the analysis of megatrends has been a constant in recent years and has triggered a new culture in the entrepreneurial field.

Megatrends also vary in different regions of the world. In Latin America in 2009, the Tecnologico de Monterrey, through a group of specialists in strategic foresight, identified 8 megatrends for the region that are still valid today and that have been accelerating as a function of the development of the region and the world. Let us now review the current status of each one of them.

1. **Green consumer.** This megatrend has been growing significantly throughout the region and in line with the world. The serious problem of climate change has led governments to provide subsidies and tax incentives to companies that promote the use of renewable energies and reduce their carbon footprint in general. On the other hand, through associations and activists in the field from different areas, has been generating awareness in society, changes in habits and ways of acting of people that creates this profile of the green consumer. A large part of the UN Sustainable Development Goals (SDGs) for the year 2030 addresses this megatrend.

2. **Personalized, lifelong, and universal education.** Access to life-long and democratized education has been growing and generating different business formats. The incorporation of information and communication technologies (ICTs) has enabled significant progress in this area. For example, MOOC's (Massive online open courses) are already a reality that impacts millions of people around the world. In Latin America, more and more universities are joining the delivery of this type of courses and companies are creating their own online courses to train their employees. It is evident that the recent pandemic accelerated this megatrend due to the need for confinement and hybrid models of education (face-to-face and virtual) will remain installed in all types of education.

3. **The world: one big shopping mall.** This megatrend has to do with the new ways of doing business, which is moving toward the unification of consumption and efficiency in the supply chain. In other words, it has to do with the use of ecommerce. Examples such as Amazon and Alibaba and their exponential growth show the rise of this megatrend. The COVID-19 pandemic has multiplied this trend, causing local and regional commerce to join this trend as well.

4. **Asset management and global governance.** It refers to the way in which resources are managed and decisions are made at a global level. It basically arises from the crisis of the current economic model, which has generated economic inequality, environmental deterioration, human rights crises, migratory flows, and other global problems beyond national governments, and which leads to thinking about new forms of global governance and economic models. We have seen that this megatrend has been reflected in a struggle between different models and forms of governance that have polarized society, from those who propose a strengthening of supranational organizations or greater international trade openness (Inter-American Court of Human Rights, UN, European Union, OECD, etc.) to those who propose the disappearance of such organizations, national government control over problems such as immigration or greater sovereignty over resources (i.e., BREXIT). This megatrend has polarized citizens around the world but has also favored the growing creation of an interest in social entrepreneurship and the drive to solve global problems.

5. **Personalized marketing.** It refers to the direct interaction between companies and consumers, that is, to have more and more specific and personal knowledge of the customer. The use of "bid data" generated by ICT, algorithms, and artificial intelligence, enhanced by the massive use of social networks and digital platforms, has generated a detailed knowledge of people (what do you see, what do you eat, where are you, where are you going, etc.) and has generated countless new companies based on the development of these platforms and the sale of this information. It has also given great visibility and transparency, but at the same time is a great invader of privacy ("big brother") leading to manipulation and cosmetic marketing. The pandemic has also driven this megatrend and led to ethical reflection on the massive use of information.

6. **New demographic and family structure.** Undoubtedly, demographic changes in Latin America represent a megatrend that allows to assertively approach the future demands of the population. Latin America is the fastest aging region in the world, the so-called demographic bonus of the region, that is, a higher percentage of productive

people in the population pyramid, will start to change from 2025 onwards. Changes in family structures, from the traditional family to the extended and diverse family, will also affect consumer habits and behaviors with the emergence of new needs. The gender perspective and feminist movements have also grown significantly (due to the inequality, physical, and sexual violence suffered by women) and open spaces toward a different society in the future.

7. **Technological health**. Refers to the impact of transferring knowledge and technological innovations in the field of medicine. The development of specialized techniques for less invasive diagnosis and healing, the use of new-generation drugs and the evolution of genetics have led to the growth of attractive health businesses and markets. The paradox is that it failed to prevent a new pandemic that is afflicting the world and will change it forever. On the other hand, this use of knowledge and technology has led to the emergence of a vaccine against the COVID-19 virus in record time and also precisely with the use of a technology that is expected to revolutionize the cure or prevention of different diseases for the good of mankind.

8. **Everyday virtuality**. This refers to the continuous use of ICTs derived from the use of the Internet and cellular telephony, which has generated different technological behaviors and habits. Phenomena such as "influencers," "YouTubers," channels, newscasts, and online streamings are examples of this change in habits. So are services that can be performed online, such as electronic banking and public services. All this has led to a proliferation of apps for all kinds of uses and in all areas of daily life. The pandemic has also boosted this virtuality by the need to work and study from home and the exponential increase in videoconferencing services and technological tools for teamwork and virtual education.

These megatrends cannot be overlooked in the context of Latin America's economic reality and social vulnerability. For example, the lack of access to broadband connectivity for large population groups means that large segments of the population are at a disadvantage or that small and medium-sized enterprises are unable to compete. A previous economic crisis in the region and the one being left by the pandemic in the increase of population in poverty makes innovation and entrepreneurship difficult. The OECD (2019), even before the global crisis due to confinement, posed four major development traps for Latin America: low productivity, social vulnerability, lack of strong institutions and intensive use of natural resources.

The challenges for the region are enormous, but there is no doubt that megatrends, largely derived from the use of information and communication technologies, have been generating large-scale, global entrepreneurship in Latin America. Business families have an advantage in the face of these megatrends because they are more entrepreneurial and generate more innovation than non-family businesses. This is largely due to their ability to become entrepreneurial families.

6.2.2 The New Generation of Entrepreneurs

One of the factors that have led to the emergence of family entrepreneurship in Latin America is the entrepreneurial intention of the new generations. According to the GUESSS Project (Global University Entrepreneurial Spirit Students' Survey) in its 2018[3] report, 34% of students worldwide want to be entrepreneurs after 5 years of graduating, while in Latin America it is notably higher at 53%. The following chart shows the data for Latin American countries in that study (Fig. 6.1).

In the chart we can see that even the Latin American country with the lowest percentage of entrepreneurship is above average. This is a result of the characteristics of the region, which has a younger population and where there is a need to promote entrepreneurship as a development factor, as there are not enough employment options.

The intention to be an entrepreneur has to do with the environment in which the new generations develop. The family context is one of them. This GUESSS 2018 study shows that 23.7% of the students come from an entrepreneurial family and when we make the relation of this factor with the action of entrepreneurship shows these elements as determinants. In other words, the transmission of the knowledge of

---

[3] Survey made to 54 countries, at more than 3000 universities, and generated more than 208,000 completed responses.

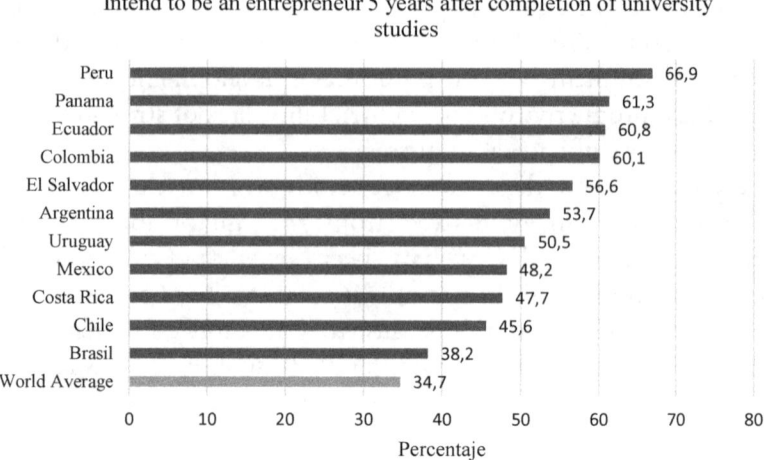

Fig. 6.1 GUESSS 2018 Survey (*Source* GUESSS 2018 Survey)

entrepreneurship from one generation to another is fundamental in the new generation of entrepreneurs.

Another contextual factor in the entrepreneurship of new generations is the entrepreneurial training provided by universities. In Latin America, the entrepreneurship courses taken by students in universities and the entrepreneurial environment they live in have a high impact on the intention to become entrepreneurs 5 years after graduation (Lopez and Alvarez, 2019).

A notable example of this impact is the one carried out by the Tecnologico de Monterrey in Mexico, which in "The Princeton Review: Top Undergraduate Schools for Entrepreneurship Ranking 2021" places it in position 5 as one of the best universities in promoting entrepreneurship. In a recent research that we were able to conduct with different colleagues (Sandoval-Arzaga et al., 2017) we showed such impact by describing the cases of three students coming from business families who created their startup in three different sectors: recycling tires, financial services, and technological development; they also came from three different degree programs: business administration, industrial engineering, and biotechnology; the results showed that the main triggers of new entrepreneurship creation in Tecnológico de Monterrey were grouped into four categories:

a. Academic content. Entrepreneurship courses across the curriculum.
b. Inspiration. Professors who ran his own company or founders of big enterprises.
c. Motivation. Focused on a desire to transcend (contributing to society) and the desire for success.
d. Support. Entrepreneurship infrastructure that the university provided (incubator), entrepreneurial family background, and the ability to form a complementary entrepreneurial team.

On the other hand, the emergence of entrepreneurs in the region, in addition to the entrepreneurial intention, has to do with the generational profile to which they belong. Undoubtedly, millennials are the new generation of entrepreneurs, who are immersed in digital technology and have lived disruptive business moments that have changed the way we relate to each other; they are also the first digital natives and therefore this highly innovative context favors them for entrepreneurship. It is said of millennials that they are diverse, idealistic, conscious, and above all that they are in search of new experiences and that they do not like to stay for a long time in the same job (Howe & Strauss, 2000), which allows them to consider the creation of new businesses as an opportunity for development in their lives. We only have to look at the numerous rankings of Latin American magazines (entrepreneurs, expansion, business, and entrepreneurship) or universities (MIT innovators under 35) that currently proliferate about successful young Latin American entrepreneurs as a model for success in our current society.

We have already mentioned that the difficult economic conditions and the great inequalities in the Latin American region have been factors in the drive of governments and institutions to train new generations as entrepreneurs. Many young people in the world and in particular in emerging or developing economies, such as most countries in Latin America, when they graduate do not have a job or it is precarious. In 2017 it was estimated that 70.9 million young people in the world were unemployed being the unemployment rate of 13.1% and even in OECD countries about 18% of unemployed youth did not have a job for a year or more, being 76.7% of youth work informal.[4] These alarming data have led one of the Sustainable Development Goals (SDG) for 2030 proposed by the UN to be decent work and economic growth and to achieve it one of the key strategies is to promote entrepreneurship among young people. The idea is to ensure that more and more new generations can generate their own businesses, improve their quality of life, and provide jobs. Encouraging entrepreneurship also contributes to achieving SDG number 1, which is no poverty, and that is why Latin American governments are aware of the need to create an entrepreneurial ecosystem that includes policies to optimize the regulatory environment, promote awareness and networking, improve access to finance, facilitate technology exchange and innovation, enhance entrepreneurship education and skills development (Holt, 2020).

In Latin America, young people are increasingly becoming entrepreneurs due to the role of universities, the government, and the business family itself, which has contributed to the new wave of family entrepreneurs.

6.2.3 Learning to Be an Entrepreneur Inside the Business Family

Entrepreneurship is a necessity for every business family for at least three reasons: it improves the economic performance of the company, increases the probability of continuity of the business family, and opens development opportunities for new generations. However, achieving this is not an easy process and many business families fail in the attempt. The story of Adidas and Puma, two brothers who managed to successfully start their businesses, but which led to a family breakup, is well known.

Therefore, it is important for entrepreneurial families to develop the ability to learn entrepreneurship as a family in order to create not only economic value but also family cohesion. Some of the key elements in

---

[4] ILO (2017) Global Employment Trends for Youth 2017. International Labor Organization. https://www.ilo.org/wcmsp5/groups/public/---dgreports/---dcomm/---publ/documents/publication/wcms_598669.pdf.

which this ability of entrepreneurial families to enhance entrepreneurship between generations is shown (Sandoval-Arzaga et al., 2021) are described below.

Motivation. Without motivation there is no action. The success of the entrepreneurial action must be based on unraveling the motives and genuine aspirations of the new entrepreneurs. Nowadays, the motivation of the new generations for entrepreneurship is not only to be economically successful, but also to generate solutions that have a positive impact on society (environment, economic and social inequality, diversity, and human rights). New generations should not be pressured to undertake what previous generations want. Undertaking something they are not truly motivated to do just for the sake of commitment or to get along with other family members usually kills the entrepreneurial impulse.

Inspiration. It all starts with inspiration. Inspiration does not come from magic but fundamentally from other people. It is said that entrepreneurial families already have the "entrepreneurial gene" because the generations are growing up in continuous contact with what it means to make a company. But this is enhanced when the stories are documented and the anecdotes of the founders or entrepreneurial leaders who have created the businesses are told. It is also important to have direct contact with other entrepreneurs outside the family who are becoming role models. Documenting and talking about the stories of family entrepreneurship and taking advantage of the contacts of the business family to approach and learn from other entrepreneurs (not from the family) are a source of inspiration.

Family Entrepreneurship Lab. Fail, test, and get it right. The best methodologies for entrepreneurship today are those that validate and iterate ideas with customers over and over again until the right solution is found. The resources of the family business, the network of contacts, and the economic capital should be an advantage for family entrepreneurship. But it is only so if it is consciously put at the service of new entrepreneurial projects. The entrepreneurial families that already have the infrastructure in place can organize all these resources, set the rules, and create the formal spaces for the new generations to undertake. This can be called the family entrepreneurship lab. In this laboratory, ideas are incubated, business models are tested, and the seed capital necessary for entrepreneurship is provided.

Entrepreneurial family team. The team is the basis for learning. Learning to become a business family is only possible if the entrepreneurial family forms a learning team, that is to say, if it is capable of combining the different ideas, expectations, experiences, and knowledge of the different family members from different generations to achieve synergy. It is possible to achieve this if there is adequate communication and family dynamics. The main objective of this team is to be a guide, support, and compass for family entrepreneurs. The generations that lead the family business must give space and empower the new generations to foster their self-esteem and show results. The new generations must be a "sponge" to learn the experiences of the previous ones and be humble to ask for help. It is a space for sharing and integrating knowledge among the different generations where the family openly discusses the emotions and problems of their entrepreneurial projects.

Developing family entrepreneurship requires, from the business family, to put into play these four elements in one way or another to create a culture of transgenerational entrepreneurship, as we mentioned at the beginning of this chapter, and to bear the necessary fruits to move from a family business to an entrepreneurial family.

Another fundamental element that must be taken into account for entrepreneurship to work within the family is to provide adequate governance on the part of the entrepreneurial family so that this entrepreneurship can take place. Governance for family entrepreneurship means establishing direction in the family business system for proper decision-making to foster entrepreneurship. The elements that entrepreneurial families should consider in order to establish this governance are:

a. Purpose and values. Define the sense and reason for promoting the family business and that both are aligned with the values of the entrepreneurial family. For example, if the new product or service to be undertaken has a high impact on the environment and this contravenes the values of the entrepreneurial family.
b. Types of Entrepreneurships. The aim is to define the types of entrepreneurships that the family business is willing to promote.

There may be *related entrepreneurship*, i.e., which are part of or related to the main business and have strategic or value chain overlaps; or *unrelated entrepreneurship*, which are not part of the family business and serve different products and markets.

c. Ownership of the new business. It consists of establishing whether the entrepreneurial family, the company, the entrepreneur, some members of the family, or outsiders will be owners of the new entrepreneurship, and in what percentage of shares. These should be established according to the type of entrepreneurship being under-taken, whether related or unrelated. For example, for an unrelated entrepreneurship the family member proposing the entrepreneurship will own 51% of the business, the entrepreneurial family (not the business) will own the other 49%. Or, if it is related, the business will have 60% and the family entrepreneur 40%.

d. Entrepreneurship process. It is about defining and making known the process of the entrepreneurship, which usually consists of following the steps of ideation, making the business model, designing a proto-type, validating it with the market, and iterating the solutions. Once certain requirements are met then it is presented to the person who will evaluate the entrepreneurship to approve it or not and establish the next steps.

e. Tracking and advising to the entrepreneur. This consists of establishing whether the family business or the company will provide support and advice for the entrepreneur to develop the entrepreneurial process from ideation to iteration or in which steps. Some families may assign mentors or establish a council, they may also have an internal laboratory or incubator, or they may provide resources for the entrepreneur, for example, to enroll in a university Business Incubator.

f. Evaluation of the entrepreneurship. Define who should evaluate the entrepreneurship. If it will be a committee of experts in which family members participate or not, if it is the board of directors or a committee of the company, or if it is the family shareholders or the family council, among others. This evaluation committee usually establishes a recommendation, whether the entrepreneurship should be approved or not, or if it requires further validation by the entrepreneur.

g. Choice of the entrepreneurship. This consists of establishing who or what body should be the one to approve or not the entrepreneurship. They may be the same or different from those mentioned in the evaluation process. It also refers to establishing who makes the decision or who should validate it. For example, for a decision on a related entrepreneurship, it can be established that the company's innovation committee will follow up, the entrepreneurship committee of the board of directors will approve it, and the family council will validate it.

h. Source of financing of the entrepreneurship. This involves defining the sources of financing for the entrepreneurship: whether it will be a direct contribution to share capital; whether it will be a loan from the entrepreneurial family's fund; whether it will be from the company's new business fund or from an external source such as bank loans or governmental support.

i. Start-up of the entrepreneurship. This consists of defining who should follow up, evaluate, and advise that the entrepreneurship is being carried out, that the objectives of the launching plan are met, that the entrepreneur is asked for accounts and results, and at the same time that he/she is advised and supported to reach a successful conclusion with the entrepreneurship. They can be some of the same people or instances described in the evaluation or election, that is to say, a committee of experts in which family members participate or not, or if it is the board of directors or a committee of the company, or if it is the family shareholders or the family council, among others.

j. Exit procedure or failure of the entrepreneurship. This consists of establishing the exit rules in the event that any of the proposed shareholders of the new entrepreneurship no longer wish to continue, as well as making clear what would happen in the event that the entrepreneurship fails and it is not decided to continue. This usually involves risk and can be measured. If it is an unrelated entrepreneurship and has the objective of boosting the entrepreneurial spirit of the new generations, then the business families allocate a certain amount of non-repayable support (which does not recover the investment) or angel investors in the early stages of development of the entrepreneur-ship. In case of being related and that the company is a shareholder, the evaluation tends to be more rigorous, it is safer, but even so, from the fund of new projects, the range that is destined for the support of the same is established.

It is advisable that all of the elements described above be translated into policies and criteria for entrepreneurship, which are usually annexed to the family constitution or protocol, or to a separate entrepreneurship manual.

Encouraging entrepreneurship between generations in the right way and laying the foundations, rules, and policies, i.e., the governance of entrepreneurship is essential for a family business to become from within an entrepreneurship family.

6.3   The Challenges of Latin American Entrepreneurial Families: Balance and Dualities

The challenge for Latin American family businesses to develop a high potential for transgenerational entrepreneurship is to find an adequate balance between financial wealth and socioemotional wealth (Cruz & Jiménez, 2017). To achieve the above, the duality between exploration and exploitation must be overcome; something called organizational ambidexterity (March, 1991). Exploration activities focus on innova-tion, i.e., searching for new opportunities, experimenting with different innovation formulas, and being flexible; while exploitation refers to the management of the opportunities found with emphasis on execution and efficiency (March, 1991).

There are two ways to be an entrepreneur in a family business. One is to be an intra-entrepreneur, that is, to develop an internal project within the family business, something called corporate entrepreneurship, where a new value proposition is generated or new clients are found; it can also be done through the acquisition of businesses that dynamize the family business. There are many examples of intra-company expansion in Latin America, such as those carried out by the Family Groups or Multilatinas described in another chapter of this book. This is the way, for example, in which Grupo Bimbo (Mexico), CENCOSUD (Chile), Tenaris (Argentina-Mexico), and Companhia Brasileira (Brazil) have grown. Intrapreneurship is therefore solving the exploration/exploitation duality by taking new ideas and innovation (exploration) from within the family business itself or by making acquisitions of other companies and taking advantage of their capacity for execution, operation, and resources (exploitation) that the Family Business Group already has.

The other way in which business families develop entrepreneurship is by promoting entrepreneurs within or outside the same family who are developing start-ups or even through spin off or split out. Exploration is then achieved through leadership, governance, and processes established by the family business. An example of how to build a successful ecosystem for entrepreneurship in Latin America is that proposed by Lozano-Posso and Urbano (2017). By studying different business families in the region that created new companies led by them, he proposes that through the Family Council and the Board, an Entrepreneurial Projects Committee is created whose objective is to evaluate and filter entrepreneurship projects, provide financial resources to fund new projects, provide infrastructure and knowledge (mentoring) to accompany family entrepreneurs, and connect with services and resources of the environment to make such project a reality. A notable example of family entrepreneurship in Latin America is Organización Espinosa (Colombia), which has created some 50 companies since 2005 and 12% have survived, according to Santiago Perry, President of the Family Council of the company and member of the fourth generation:

The number one friend of business families is entrepreneurship because the more they will survive over time; the faster families usually grow, faster than businesses. Families that have a greater appetite for risk sacrifice dividends to drive new businesses. You have to build the best possible shareholder (entrepreneurial and responsible) and not the best CFO or CEO of the company. In my company, the founders decided that the members of the following generations could not work in the company but could be owners of their own businesses, so they created a seed fund to promote them, a committee was created and from there new companies have emerged.[5]

Entrepreneurship of new businesses from outside the family business and through family shareholders involves managing the exploration/exploitation duality, encouraging start-up entrepreneurship of the new generations (exploration), and transferring the execution and operation resources of the family business (exploitation) to support the new business to operate.

The challenge for business families is to establish an ambidextrous leadership that can orchestrate the exploration/exploitation duality and combine the entrepreneurial mindset with strategic execution. Family businesses in Latin America still need to improve the balance of this duality, as shown in the study by Cruz and Jimenez (2017) of 200 Latin American family businesses that shows us that ambidextrous organizations are in Mexico 48.5%, Ecuador 45%, Chile 41.4%, Peru 35.3%, and Colombia 28.6%. Another important challenge is to adequately manage the duality between socioemotional and financial wealth, which also shows variations in Latin American countries in the different dimensions of socioemotional wealth. On average, Mexico has the highest socioemotional wealth, followed by Peru, Ecuador, Chile, and Colombia.

Latin American business families are heterogeneous, as they have a different management and leadership in family entrepreneurship, as well as in the balance of these dualities for family entrepreneurship that is located between tradition and innovation.

6.4 Case Studies

6.4.1 Fernando Fischmann: Crystal Lagoons

A global entrepreneur from an entrepreneurial family is Fernando Fischmann, a Chilean who has created a tourist and real estate complex

---

[5] Taken from the podcast Ep. 26 The DNA of the entrepreneurial family. Business Territory. Instituto de Familias Empresarias para México y Latinoamérica del Tecnológico de Monterrey. https://ifem.tec.mx/es/podcast.

with lagoons of excellent water quality and ecological, by consuming less water, energy and not using chemicals. He has offices in 15 countries and has 600 lagoons and 1500 patents in 190 countries.

Fernando Fischmann, who studied biochemistry at the University of Chile, was developing an entrepreneurial spirit since he worked in the family business (a restaurant business) and then with his sister entered the real estate business. In the mid-80s he bought a property in Algarrobo, on the coast of central Chile, where he built an apartment complex, since the sea was extremely dangerous, he came up with the idea of building a Crystal Lagoon. Like any entrepreneurial business, he went through the exploration phase, having to "pivot" his idea and test it until he got the business model right. In the first lagoon of this complex the technology failed, and it only lasted 15 days, so he had to start looking for other suppliers and alternative technologies. Fernando recalls that those were very difficult days and the owners of the apartments were not happy. While he found the solution, he built pools at the edge of the lagoon so that the owners could relax.

To find a solution he traveled to different countries around the world: Australia, Hawaii, and even Disney in Orlando, but everywhere he was told that his idea of building lagoons with that crystalline level of water was unfeasible and almost impossible. He spent 3 years trying to find the technology. Seeing that there was no one to do it, he decided to create his own laboratory at home. As in all entrepreneurships, in this phase of exploration and invention, people did not believe in him and told him he was throwing his money away.

First, he tried to improve the existing technology but after two years without results he decided that the best route was to invent his own. Thus, he obtained his first patents to achieve the turquoise color in his lagoons. He developed a different method to carry out filtration for large volumes of water while saving energy, then designed a patented natural solution for water treatment using 100 times less chemicals than traditional technologies.

The next step was to test it in the lagoon on a large scale and the result was "magical" in his own words, as it was successful because the lagoon water remained crystal clear. As the days went by, another technical problem arose with the plastic film at the bottom of the lagoon, but with a U.S. firm he developed a different mixture that solved the complication. This allowed him to develop his business model and he managed to triple the construction of apartments in his first location, where his sister was the General Manager.

By 2006, Fernando Fischmann had already developed his business concept and patented his technology in 160 countries, that is, he was able to move from the exploration phase to the exploitation phase. He generated a global plan to expand his business in Latin America, Dubai, and the United States. He also hired companies that improved his management practices and achieved great free publicity by winning the Guinness award for having the largest swimming pool, which allowed him not to invest in advertising and to get orders from all over the world to build swimming pools.

His technological developments have allowed him to join the megatrend of green business and he has developed a whole concept of a sustainable vision of water to reduce the environmental impact in different productive sectors. An example of this is a technology for cooling thermoelectric plants with an artificial lagoon. His entrepreneurial streak leads him to develop new business models, such as bringing crystalline lagoons for public use in urban areas to promote social inclusion, leisure activities, and water saving.

In 2020, because of COVID-19 their Crystal Lagoons business was one of those that did not suffer losses. Its facilities were full, even those for public use, as Crystal Lagoon could have strict sanitary control of the lagoons and access control of people. Fernando Fischmann's real estate business is one of the largest in the world and he is already preparing the transition to the new generations: he has two sons under 30 years of age who are already part of the company's board.

6.4.2 Rene Freudenberg: Interlub

Interlub was founded in 1984 by Peter Freudenberg, of German origin, when he realized that in Mexico it was difficult to find lubricants that would extend the useful life of certain types of heavy machinery. For Rene Freudenberg, Peter's son and President of Grupo Interlub, his father taught him that it was not necessary to copy technology but to develop it and, from there, go out into the world. This philosophy is at the core of Interlub and has allowed it to become an innovative global company that exports to 37 countries.

Interlub is a successful example that has managed to overcome the challenge of the exploration vs. exploitation duality and find its balance. Its exploration model is focused on innovation and the search for opportunities in specific market niches. "We seek to conquer global macro-niches," says René. The key to their development is to go against the grain of their competitors who focus on standardizing their products. Interlub, on the other hand, develops a product for each type of industry and client. To achieve this, they first identify the niche, then generate the idea, and carry out the development in their Technology Center, analyzing the operating conditions and product configuration. They have generated close to 80 new products for different markets and industries in 37 countries. To develop these disruptive technologies, they have opened research projects in collaboration with higher education institutions such as the Massachusetts Institute of Technology (MIT), Instituto Politécnico Nacional (IPN-Mexico), and Universidad Nacional Autónoma de México (UNAM).

Its operating model, that is, the successful execution and exploitation of opportunities, is divided into three major business lines: Interglass, specialized in the glass industry; Intermol, dedicated to the production of release agents for the plastics industry; and Interlub, for heavy industry such as steel, mining, and railroads, among others. Its value proposition consists of offering documented benefits and success stories of its products. For example, as of 2017 it had documented more than 1 million 300 thousand dollars annually in productivity increases, 250 thousand dollars in maintenance savings, and 71% reduction in lubricant consumption in key applications of its different customers. Working closely with the maintenance engineers of the companies it serves is part of its service capacity, in which each customer is unique and is offered customized solutions.

René Freudenburg has the firm conviction, absorbed from his father, that medium-sized family businesses are the basis for the growth of the economy and the generation of progress and transformation of countries. This is part of the German "mittlelstand" philosophy, because such companies can be more flexible, innovative, international, and humane than large companies. Family owners usually do not have to hide in anonymity, but proudly engage with all their stakeholders and extend the positive values of the family to the entire organization. "All the company's employees are one big family, a human group that goes beyond," says René, where technology, quality, and training are the cornerstones of their success.

And it is precisely this type of leadership that has allowed Interlub to be an example in the balance of the exploration–exploitation model, as it maintains a remarkable balance between growth and a human-centered organizational culture. This entrepreneurial family business encourages knowledge transfer among its employees, collective intelligence, and a horizontal structure that allows it to co-create disruptive solutions for its clients.

6.5   Chapter Summary

In this chapter we analyze the concept of family entrepreneurship as one of the keys to the continuity of family businesses in Latin America and the world. In particular, family entrepreneurship in Latin America has been triggered by three elements: social and technological megatrends, a new generation of entrepreneurs, and the capacity of family businesses to become entrepreneurial families.

The social and technological megatrends have been accelerated in general by the COVID-19 pandemic that we have had to live this year and where precisely this new profile of family entrepreneurs, usually millennials, have taken the lead and in Latin America stand out for their high intention to undertake and generate new businesses.

The challenge for Latin American entrepreneurial families is to adequately manage and balance the duality of exploration and exploitation, and here we were able to compare the differences between different countries in the Latin American region in this respect as an element of their heterogeneity.

Finally, we were able to see two notable examples of Latin American global family entrepreneurs: Fernando Fischmann and René Freudenberg, who have successfully led their organizations through innovation and technological development.

References

Allen, M. R., & Gartner, W. B. (2021). *Family entrepreneurship*. Springer.

Brenes, E., & Haar, J. (2012). *The future of entrepreneurship in Latin America*. Springer.

Brenes, E., Fonseca-Paredes, M., Jiménez, G., Marzano, G., & Nordqvist, M. (2011). *Understanding entrepreneurial family business in uncertain environments*. Edward Elgar Publishing.

Crystal Lagoons: El verano pandémico disparó el negocio de Fischman. *NexNews*. http://portal.nexnews.cl/showN?valor=fej9s.

Cruz, C., & Jiménez, I. (2017). *Latin American entrepreneur families: How to increase cross-generational potential?* (White paper). Credit Suisse Group AG.

Fernando Fischmann, fundador de Crystal Lagoons y su visión sustentable del uso del agua. Article by Gabriel Angulo Cáceres. El mostrador. May, 2016. https://www.elmostrador.cl/agenda-pais/vida-en-linea/2016/05/16/fernando-fischmann-grandes-lagunas-artificiales-con-una-vision-sustentable/.

Habbershon, T. G., & Williams, M. L. (1999). A resource-based framework for assessing the strategic advantages of family firms. *Family Business Review, 12*(1), 1–25.

Habbershon, T. G., Nordqvist, M., & Zellweger, T. M. (2010). Transgenerational entrepreneurship. In M. Nordqvist & T. M. Zellweger (Eds.), *Transgenerational entrepreneurship: Exploring growth and performance in family firms across generations* (pp. 1–38). Edward Elgar Publishing.

Hernández-Linares, R., & López-Fernández, M. C. (2018). Entrepreneurial orientation and the family firm: Mapping the field and tracing a path for future research. *Family Business Review, 31*(3), 318–351.

Holt, D. (2020). *Exploring youth entrepreneurship*. Department of Economic and Social Affairs, United Nations. https://sdgs.un.org/es/node/24572.

Howe, N., & Strauss, W. (2000). *Millennials rising: The next great generation*. Vintage.

La expansión sin escala de Fernando Fischmann. October, 2014. AMCHAM Chile. https://www.amchamchile.cl/2014/10/la-expansion-sin-escala-de-fer nando-fischmann-2/.

Las megatendencias sociales actuales y su impacto en la identificación de oportunidades estratégicas de negocios. Grupo de Desarrollo Regional del Tecnológico de Monterrey. 2009.

Latin American Economic Outlook. (2017/2016). *Youth, skills and entrepreneurship*. OECD Publishing.

La transición que prepara Fernando Fischmann en Crystal Lagoons. Article by Mateo Navas. Diario Financieron. https://www.df.cl/noticias/df-mas/por dentro/la-transicion-que-prepara-fernando-fischmann-en-crystal-lagoons/ 2020-11-26/183722.html.

Lopez, T., & Alvarez, C. (2019). Influence of university-related factors on students' entrepreneurial intentions. *International Journal of Entrepreneurial Venturing, 11*(6), 521–540.

Lozano-Posso, M., & Urbano, D. (2017). Factores relevantes en el proceso de socializacion, vinculacion y pertenencia de descendientes en empresas familiares. *Revista Innovar, 27*(63), 61–77.

Lumpkin, G. T., & Dess, G. G. (1996). Clarifying the entrepreneurial orien tation construct and linking it to performance. *Academy of Management Review, 21*, 135–172.

March, J. G. (1991). Exploration and exploitation in organizational learning. *Organization Science, 2*, 71–87.

Mata Ferrusquía, Ruth. *La empresa mexicana que triunfó llevando la contra a su sector*. En Forbes. https://www.forbes.com.mx/la-empresa-mexicana-que triunfo-llevando-la-contra-a-su-sector/.

Miller, D. (1983). The correlates of entrepreneurship in three types of firms. *Management Science, 29*, 770–791.

Mo, A., & de Haro Rodríguez, G. (2017). *Millennials, la generación emprende dora*. Grupo Planeta.

Moori Koening, V. (2004). *Desarrollo emprendedor*. IDB.

Müller, C., Botero, I., Discua, A., & Subramanian, R. (2018). *Family firms in Latin America*. Routledge.

Naisbitt, J., & Aburdene, P. (1990). *Megatrends 2000: Ten new directions for the 1990s*. New York: William Morrow & Company.

Nájar, D. (2010). Emprendedores emergentes. LID Editorial empresarial.

Perspectivas de la OCDE en Ciencia, Tecnología e Innovación. 2016.

Perspectivas económicas de América Latina. (2019). Desarrollo en transición: Desarrollo en transición. OECD, Economic Commission for Latin America and the Caribbean, CAF Development Bank of Latin America, European Union. OECD Publishing.

Premio nacional de calidad. manufactura. (2017). Interlub Group. https://www.pnc.org.mx/wp-content/uploads/Ganadoras2017/Interlub-PNC-2017-min.pdf.

Price, J. (2017). 5 megatendencias en Latinoamérica. Su impacto económico, social y político. Americas Market Intelligence (AMI).

Sandoval-Arzaga, F., González, D. S. X., Silveyra, G., & Fonseca-Paredes, M. (2017). Contextualizing universities for new venture creation: the case of family business students at the Tecnologico de Monterrey in Mexico. In *Contextualizing entrepreneurship in emerging economies and developing countries*. Edward Elgar Publishing.

Sandoval-Arzaga, F., Silveyra, G., & Xotlanihua-González, D. S. (2021). Gathering multiple generations at the dining room: The Secret Toward an Entrepreneurial Family Continuity. In *Family entrepreneurship: Insights from leading experts on successful multi-generational entrepreneurial families* (p. 213).

Schwab, K. (2016). *La cuarta revolución industrial*. Penguin Random House.

Sieger, P., Fueglistaller, U., Zellweger, T., & Braun, I. (2018). *Global student entrepreneurship 2018: Insights from 54 countries* (Global GUESSS Report, 3). St. Gallen/Bern: KMU-HSG/IMU.

7

Conclusions, Lessons Learned, and New Avenues for Further Research

During the last two decades, there has been a growing interest in the study of family businesses and their interrelation with other specialties and sciences, such as anthropology and sociology, and this incorporation is undoubtedly a relevant contribution to the knowledge we have of this ownership structure. Much of the current research has focused on comparing family businesses with non-family businesses; in other cases, on the dynamics of family businesses according to their size, or on analyzing them as individual businesses, not as a more homogeneous group. Other groups of scholars have been concerned with unraveling the relationship between family performance or issues related to corporate governance and other transgenerational issues such as succession, leaving out the roots of the family and how it affects the evolution of the business with its environment. From this point of view, the contributions we make with this text and its historical perspective led us to review, from the origin of Latin American civilization, which are those family resources that have been transmitted from generation to generation and how this legacy has been shaped by the historical evolution of societies, building a unique type of social capital. This evolutionary

© The Author(s), under exclusive license to Springer Nature
Switzerland AG 2021
C. G. Müller and F. Sandoval-Arzaga, *Family Business Heterogeneity
in Latin America*, Palgrave Studies in Family Business Heterogeneity,
https://doi.org/10.1007/978-3-030-78931-2_7

dynamic can explain, for example, the differences that affect performance or continuity in the short and long term.

Family businesses in Latin America are composed of diverse and varied characteristics that make them different from their peers in the world, but also among the different countries of the American continent. And this is what gives a heterogeneous character to the family business in Latin America.

In this book we have made an effort to describe in a simplified, clear, and simple way all this diverse nature through different moments over time in something we have called waves. Knowing each wave represents the evolution of family businesses in the American continent and, in a way, the characteristics of each wave nurtures and blends with the next to enrich it and give family businesses the melting pot of which Latin American society is composed.

7.1   A Summary of the Characteristics of Each Wave

7.1.1 First Wave—"The Syncretism"

The pre-Columbian period and the early years of the colony encompass this period (before 1492 until the 1700s approximately). The Latin American family business is heterogeneous by nature and this is due to the emergence of the Latin American concept based on the mixture and adoption of beliefs and ways of life between the pre-Columbian peoples and Latin Europe, mainly Spanish and Portuguese, which was later joined by the African, reflected in racial and cultural miscegenation.

The first "family businesses" in the continent were pre-Columbian since they were based on domestic production with a family self-sufficiency base that we can refer to today as a Family Team (Gimeno et al., 2010) that works with high dedication to the service of the company. Before the appearance of the first large pre-Columbian urban centers, the simile of the first "Family Groups" also arose, where extended families or family branches joined together to produce the surplus needed by the population through diverse economic activities and with hierarchical control. In colonial times, the first family businesses were those of merchants and landowners who were a hegemonic oligopoly that took advantage of relations with the crown and maintained the privileges of domination prevailing in New Spain.

The cultural heritage of this wave is reflected today in: indigenous entrepreneurship, products and services of pre-Columbian origin that result in the economic development of their community; the n-Culturales, the integration of different identities and cultures that enhance their business capabilities; and the formation of large oligopolistic family economic groups that have as their antecedents the haciendas and large estates of the colony. The family businesses of the time have also contributed to the social and economic progress of Latin American countries.

7.1.2 Second Wave—First Migration Flows

The colonial legacy that dominated the so-called Spanish Indies developed for almost 300 years, from the time of colonization (1492) and until the processes of emancipation and independence (depending on the Latin American country around 1810). During this period, migration flows gave life to this region of the world where 65% of the population descends from migrants and in regions where the concentration of native peoples is denser, such as Bolivia, Peru, Honduras, Guatemala, or the south of Mexico, this figure rises to more than 80%.

This condition is reflected in the strong heterogeneity of the current family businesses that we can observe in the region. In fact, the cases presented in the book of the Dimare, Nishimura, and Freudenberg families are clear examples of these migration flows. This cultural diversity (from the origin) is as wide as the decisions in their governance structures, resources, and divergent objectives. This behavior is reflected in the way of thinking, feeling, acting, in the traits of the culture and, of course, in the way of doing business.

The economic system of this colonial period was strongly based on mining operations, which together with the taxes and tributes that had to be paid to the Crown of Spain and Portugal, made the development of a society with average standards unfeasible, in addition to the high costs of imports from Europe. Economic supremacy was dominated by the treasury and the merchants who ensured the link with the Peninsula. It is difficult to identify the long-lived families during this period that managed to last for more generations, but there is no doubt that many of them were linked to the power exercised by the control of Spain or Portugal. Some of these families are Hacienda Los Lingues of Chile and Grupo Cuervo of Mexico. Thus, we see three types of entrepreneurial families from the sixteenth to the eighteenth century: those migrants of Spanish or Portuguese origin who obtained a permit to cultivate the land—encomenderos—; other migrants of diverse origins who, based on a trade, managed to make their way in society by producing goods or services; and a third group of merchants who knew the foreign trade system of the time with the approval of the colonizing Kingdoms.

Thus, the foundational process of the first entrepreneurial families in Latin America was established under these migration flows, which is a source of social capital creation and lays the foundations for moral behavior and cooperation. The family is an institution that contributes to shaping the attitudes and behaviors of its members and, consequently, has a clear effect on the generation of the social capital of the family business. The family and the business are generalized among individuals who integrate shared visions and norms that must be respected and that are passed on from generation to generation. These behaviors promote the emergence of cooperative initiatives and mutually beneficial collective actions (Kwon & Adler, 2014). This value background is founded with one's own family history and culture (Carr et al., 2016).

7.1.3 The Third Wave: Mapping the Formation of the Family Group

This wave presents the development of family businesses in Latin America and the sources of heterogeneity from the analysis, creation, and development of large Latin American family conglomerates.

Although this condition has been previously studied, it fails to connect its evolution or explain its origin, which is linked to the diversity of the realities of each country. Seen in perspective, Latin American countries share many similar characteristics in their productive systems, such as the exploitation of commodities and natural resources which, in general, are heterogeneous industries, but of low productivity, as well as the common presence of a very large informal economy in the context of weak state capacities. This has generated divergent capitalist socioeconomic regimes, in some countries of the region operating through reliance on markets to organize value creation and wealth distribution and in others through the mediating role of socio-political commitments, embedded in a series of more robust institutional forms, which encourage entrepreneurship and wealth creation. These criteria have led to classify the region into four types of capitalism: international outsourcing—as in the case of Mexico and other Central American countries-, socio developmentalist—as in Brazil with a domestic consumption rate well above the economies of the region-, rentier/liberal—as in the case of Chile and Uruguay, and rentier/redistributive—as in Venezuela, Ecuador and Bolivia- (Bizberg, 2019).

We thus see a region where the rules of the game have been heterogeneous. The incorporation of the concept of institutions as a determinant of individual behaviors represents a great influence on the performance of the economy, so this section focused on comprehending societies and their economic systems through the set of choices that individuals have to make decisions and therefore the family businesses that operate, develop or die.

An example of the above is the decision that family businesses in the region have made to become more competitive and be among the best global players. Many family businesses in the region have made the decision to professionalize their processes and hire talent from outside the family. This decision has not been without ambition, optimism and patience and a long-term view. The moment at which the few family businesses decide to internationalize will depend on several factors. This process is slower compared to non-family businesses, but in the long run, the degree achieved is almost the same. The explanation is that family owners are likely to be reluctant to build relationships in foreign networks, even if they speak the same language and have similar customs. They may require higher levels of knowledge in their local market before opening up to international markets.

7.1.4 The Fourth Wave: The New Wave of Global Family Entrepreneurs

Family entrepreneurship is the key to the continuity of family businesses today. In Latin America, global entrepreneurial families have emerged in contrast to the formation of the large family groups of the previous wave.

The factors that trigger this phenomenon are the social and technological megatrends in Latin America, many of them exacerbated today by the COVID-19 pandemic. These are: Green consumer; personalized, lifelong and universal education; the world: one big shopping mall; asset management and global governance; personalized marketing; new demographic and family structure; technological health; and everyday virtuality. Another factor is the entrepreneurial profile and intention of the new generations, which has increased significantly in Latin America compared to other countries in the world. Finally, family businesses have learned to develop and educate family entrepreneurs and have become entrepreneurial families.

The challenges faced by family businesses in relation to family entrepreneurship have to do with the right balance between the exploration and exploitation of new business models and their ability to manage the duality between economic and socioemotional well-being. This balance and these dualities are managed differently in different Latin American countries, which makes the region's entrepreneurial families heterogeneous.

The following figure shows the development of the four waves (Fig. 7.1):

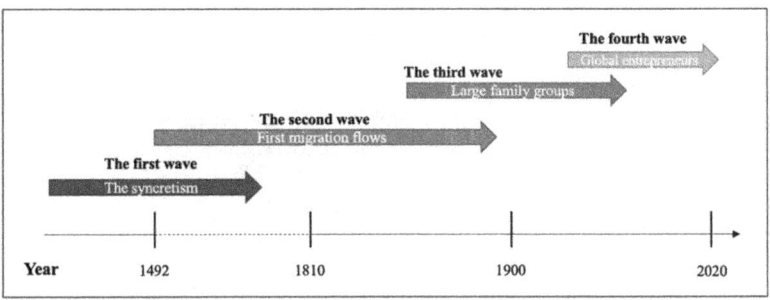

Fig. 7.1 The four waves, sources of heterogeneity

7.2   Explanatory Tables and Quadrants

With the following tables and quadrants, we seek to graphically show the heterogeneous elements as a way of contributing to the appreciation of diversity and Latin American family businesses based on the research we have carried out for the construction of this book (Fig. 7.2).

It is important to say that each of the waves does not replace the other, but on the contrary adds its elements of diversity to the next, which makes Latin American family businesses incredibly heterogeneous and gives them a great richness given their cultural heritage and their great strength in their social capital. The cases we have described in the different chapters add in their history a combination of the diverse characteristics of each wave.

For example, Grupo Cuervo comes from (Fig. 7.3 and Matrix 7.1):

This matrix allows us to observe the impact that heterogeneity factors have triggered in each of the waves on their cultural heritage and on the formation of the social capital of family businesses over time.

We could establish that, just as the heterogeneity of family businesses is supported by the differences in the management control system among a class of family businesses based on the stage of the life cycle, using markets and clans (Moores & Mula, 2000), with this quadrant we can see that Latin American family businesses are heterogeneous because of their cultural heritage and the strength of their social capital. In other words, we could establish 4 types of heterogeneous Latin American family businesses:

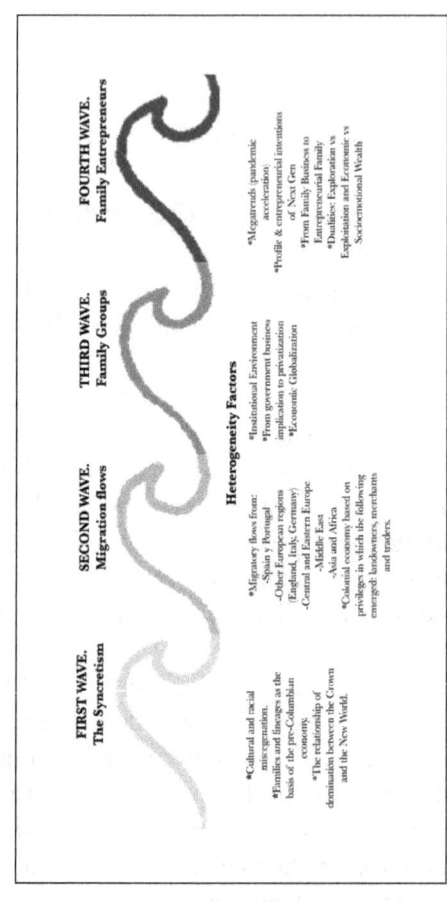

Fig. 7.2 The heterogeneity of Latin American family businesses

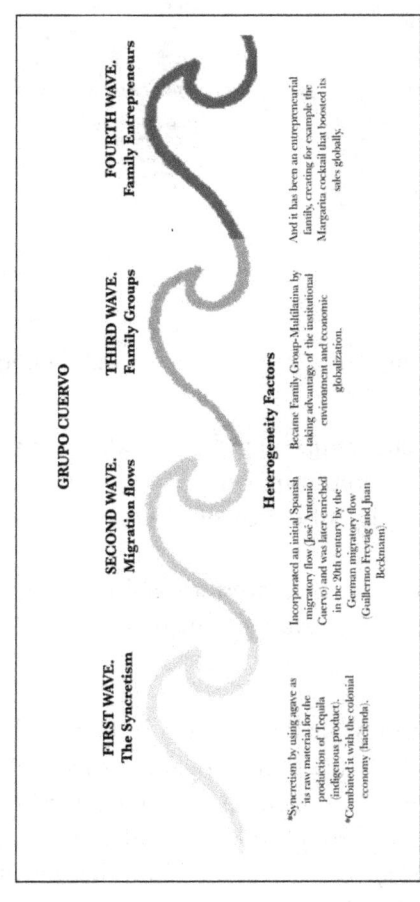

Fig. 7.3 The heterogeneity of Grupo Cuervo

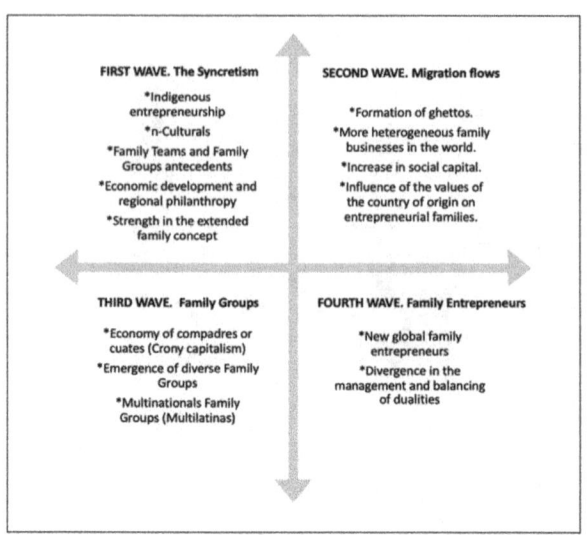

FIRST WAVE. The Syncretism

*Indigenous entrepreneurship
*n-Culturals
*Family Teams and Family Groups antecedents
*Economic development and regional philanthropy
*Strength in the extended family concept

SECOND WAVE. Migration flows

*Formation of ghettos.
*More heterogeneous family businesses in the world.
*Increase in social capital.
*Influence of the values of the country of origin on entrepreneurial families.

THIRD WAVE. Family Groups

*Economy of compadres or cuates (Crony capitalism)
*Emergence of diverse Family Groups
*Multinationals Family Groups (Multilatinas)

FOURTH WAVE. Family Entrepreneurs

*New global family entrepreneurs
*Divergence in the management and balancing of dualities

Matrix 7.1   Impact quadrant. Social capital and cultural heritage

1. Indigenous Entrepreneurship—market products or services of or taken from indigenous communities.
2. Migration Flow—strong influence of the values of the country of origin.
3. Multilatina—consolidated and international family group.
4. Global Entrepreneur—innovative business models with global impact.

In the cases and examples, we have shown in this book there is a clear illustration of each of these types of heterogeneous Latin American family businesses. For example: of Indigenous Entrepreneurship the Mapuche companies in Chile that through tourism offer a cultural experience (Macpherson et al., 2021); of Migration Flow the described case from Brazil of Jacto Group of the Nishimura family of Japanese origin; Multi-latina The Carvajal Group from Colombia; and Global Entrepreneur the case of Interlub of the Freudenberg family from Mexico (Matrix 7.2).

This matrix allows us to observe the diversity of the different Latin American countries in the first wave of the pre-Columbian era. It shows

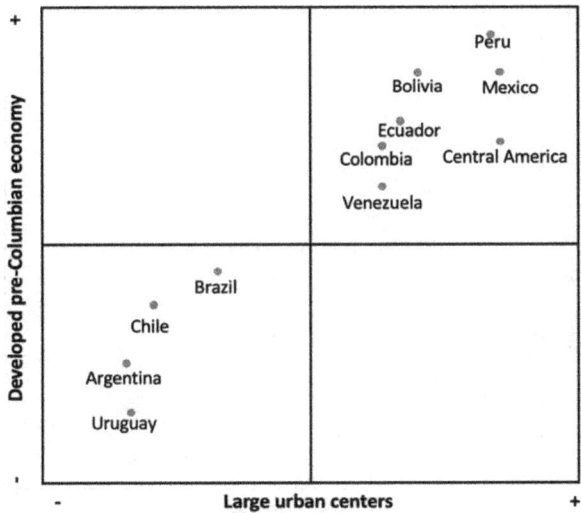

Matrix 7.2 Large urban centers and developed pre-Columbian economy

us that the largest urban centers are those related to the peoples who formed an empire such as the Incas in Peru and the Aztecs in Mexico and who controlled large regions and other peoples around them. On the other hand, this led to a major economic development of multifamily and hierarchical distributive production with a sophisticated technological infrastructure development for agriculture. Chile, Argentina, and Uruguay developed in their indigenous peoples more of a local economy based on family subsistence. This graph shows what the Spanish and Portuguese faced upon their arrival in the New World (Matrix 7.3).

This matrix allows us to infer how the level of second wave migration flows is related to differences in the quality of institutions in Latin America. We see that in a sample of ten countries there is a high level of heterogeneity between countries such as Bolivia and Chile. The first with low levels of migration where more than 65% of its inhabitants are direct descendants of indigenous peoples, but more homogeneous in groups of countries such as Mexico and Colombia or Brazil and Argentina (Matrix 7.4).

This matrix reflects the relationships in the third wave. Countries such as Bolivia, Paraguay, and Uruguay show a low level of development

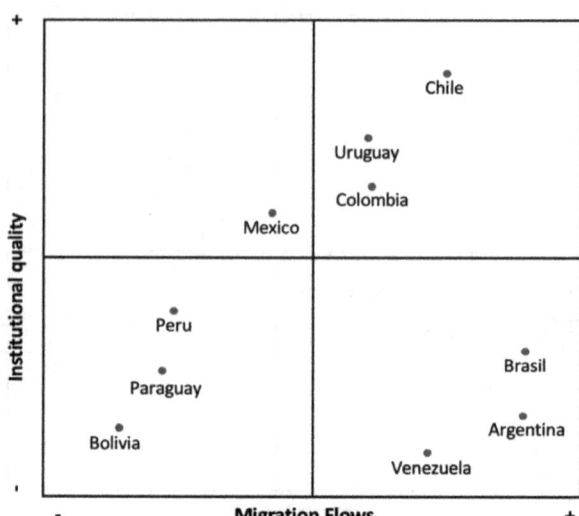

Matrix 7.3 Migration flows and institutional quality

Matrix 7.4 Number of multinational companies and family economic groups

as a multinational conglomerate and also a low level of family groups. The most emblematic case is Mexico, with an industrial and productive development history of more than 150 years that led to the development of large family-owned multinational companies such as the Slim Heliú Domit (Grupo Carso), Zambrano (Grupo Cemex), Garza Sada Laguera (FEMSA), and Garza Sada Sada (Grupo Alfa) families, all highly successful companies in their industrial sectors (Matrix 7.5).

This matrix shows the interrelationship of the fourth wave, between innovation and those who have an ambidextrous way of leading their family business. From it we can infer that the countries in which their family businesses have a better balance in managing the duality between exploration and exploitation (ambidextrous organization) can sustain themselves better over time, but they are not necessarily the most innovative, i.e., those that have created new products in the last 5 years. Family businesses in Peru and Colombia have a greater capacity to innovate and explore, but they cannot sustain themselves in the exploitation of the business model for a long time. In contrast, family businesses in Chile and Ecuador innovate less, but sustain themselves better over

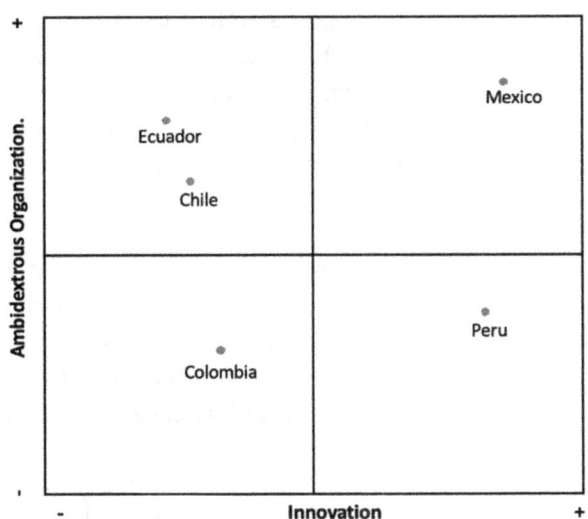

Matrix 7.5 Ambidextrous organization and innovation (*Source* Adapted from Latin American STEP Report 2019)

time. Mexico shows a middle ground between these two extremes on the innovation side, but better ambidextrous leadership.

7.3   Lessons Learned

These final lines leave us with a series of teachings and some lessons learned, after going through almost 500 years of history associated with the Latin American family business. As with any study dedicated to Latin America, given its complexity and diversity, it has been fascinating to delve into its history to unravel the origin, confirmation, and evolution of family businesses in the continent. In this section we would like to offer the reader a set of lessons learned that we have extracted from the research and elaboration of this work.

One of these lessons is that we must look at Latin American family businesses as a multicolored, diverse and heterogeneous mosaic, as are our own countries throughout the region. The richness and amalgamation of different cultures, thoughts and ways of thinking give a unique characteristic to family businesses in this region. This does not leave aside the possibility of framing certain patterns that have been shared by family businesses in Latin America and that allow us to look at them in perspective in order to extract from them the possibility of a deeper considerate of their characteristics in their different stages. As a result of our work, we propose the following characteristics that may be common to family businesses in Latin America:

(a) They are the most heterogeneous in essence. They share the syncretism and mixture of different native cultures with the cultures of the old continent, mainly Spanish and European. To this we must add the global immigration flows that the continent has experienced and that makes them the most heterogeneous in the world.
(b) The longest-lived companies are still young. If we consider that the oldest surviving family businesses were founded around 1700, they have a maximum of 13 generations. In the world there are family businesses with more than twice as many generations. On the other hand, the formation of the current family business groups occurred

in the eighties, so most Latin American family businesses are between the second and third generation.

(c) The extended family base is its strength. From pre-Columbian times to today's entrepreneurial family businesses, family support and cooperation, beyond a closed nucleus, has been a strength in the evolution of the Latin American family business.

(d) Their cultural heritage drives progress. The richness of the Latin American family business from the indigenous groups, the cultural mix, and the philanthropic contribution have driven the economic and social progress of the different regions and communities.

(e) They have a developed social capital anchored in their values. The wave of immigration that the continent experienced allowed both an increase in the social and relational capital of family businesses and the anchoring of the values of dynamic immigrant groups in the formation of ghettos.

(f) Family Business Groups concentrate most of the wealth. The phenomenon of the privatization of state-owned companies in the eighties, in line with the neoliberal economy imposed from outside, resulted in the creation of large family business groups in the continent, which have even been able to grow and position themselves as large Multilatin companies. They have grown under the protection of political power and today influence it.

(g) They have a great capacity for adaptation and resilience. Family businesses in the continent have had to navigate from the beginning with great environmental turbulences such as wars, epidemics, economic crises, corruption and political and institutional instability, which has remained as part of the culture of business families having to reinvent themselves several times through the different generations.

(h) They are global entrepreneurs. This capacity to reinvent themselves, together with technological and social megatrends and a better entrepreneurial education of the new generations, has led to the emergence of new entrepreneurial family businesses that are capable of competing with markets anywhere in the world.

We would like to emphasize that one of the most deeply rooted values is the strong entrepreneurial spirit and resilience of family businesses in this region, despite the low institutional quality and enormous variance in the rules of the game, political changes, coups d'état, and social problems. This is manifested through the opportunities they provide to their future generations by encouraging entrepreneurship and education, which results in new generations having new business opportunities and better management methodologies for the family business, adapting the conditions of their business to their markets. The most successful families use entrepreneurial action as a growth strategy. This is not without its own challenges, as the business aspirations of the older and younger generations diverge. We also see the examples of large family groups and their ability to diversify, key to staying relevant generation after generation.

As we have seen in the different sections, the characteristics of their people are vividly reflected in Latin American families and companies, they are hardworking, cheerful, resilient, flexible, creative, and concerned about social relations, with a sense of belonging to their local environment and capable of navigating complex environments. Therefore, each particular story of a family business that has survived can sometimes be seen as the story of the family business of all regions. For example, the mechanisms, practices, and decisions taken by a Peruvian family business to weather an economic crisis may reflect the similarities and commonalities of a Brazilian family business in adapting to these complex environments.

All of the above creates a character in family entrepreneurship, but without losing the sense of belonging to others, especially to their family environment. The sense of cooperativism helps to find ways to work together and align their interests, even when there are macroeconomic conflicts or succession issues and family breakdowns. The need to continue the process of building businesses is also driven by the increasing demand for wealth creation for future generations as the family grows. We have also seen, particularly in most of the eight cases presented here, the sense of caring for reputation, which many families cultivate with honor, and which plays a relevant role in the very competitiveness of Latin American family businesses, especially when they decide to embark on new challenges.

7.4   Limitations and Further Research

We would like to emphasize that research on heterogeneity and this historical retrospective is at a pioneering stage. Therefore, in this book we have sought to add a new dimension to the research agenda on family businesses in Latin America. In the study made by Colli and Fernández (2013) on Business History and Family Firms, in their review of the literature on papers that show a historical perspective of family firms, there is not a single one particular to Latin America and there are few that approach it from an international or global perspective, being in several cases analysis of some Latin American countries. Each section has focused on a wave that in itself could be the subject of future research, but there are many other areas relevant to our perception of the unique characteristics and complexities of family firms in Latin America.

We see great scope for adopting a new variety of theoretical perspectives that are currently unexplored. One example of this is the application of more sophisticated evolutionary theories to family business research. Another example is to build on the ontological dimensions of knowledge, which could consider the question of how organizational knowledge is generated, focusing on the levels of knowledge-creating entities at the individual, group, organizational, and inter-organizational levels, i.e., the environment in which knowledge is involved. This could help to understand the potential impact of knowledge flows in time series such as the ones we have covered in this text.

We also highlight the need for better methods to collect information, whether quantitative or qualitative, but in a rigorous manner. A major shortcoming when researching family businesses in Latin America is the absence of this, especially in countries where reliable sources of information are scarce or only aggregate information is available. The global and general look that we make in this book also represents a limitation to understand the depth of certain phenomena and characteristics that each country may have developed, making a zoom in on specific countries or regions of Latin America will be necessary to understand family businesses in the region.

We see many opportunities for further research on family businesses in Latin America from this book. One particular aspect relates to the problems in changing the rules of the game that families face over time as they develop their business. Research on how family businesses in the region deal with critical challenges in contexts of low institutional quality, such as corruption, institutional gaps, or deteriorating contextual frameworks, remains scarce.

We propose that research opportunities could also go in the direction of deepening the appreciation and knowledge of the four typologies of heterogeneity of Latin American family businesses that we present: (1) Indigenous Entrepreneurship, (2) Migration Flow, (3) Multilatina, and (4) Global Entrepreneur. The *Indigenous Entrepreneurship* type of family businesses are those that commercialize products and services from indigenous communities. The Latin American region has such an important wealth of handicrafts, gastronomy, culture, and tourism that to investigate and learn more about this type of family businesses rooted in traditional culture can be a driver of development and equitable progress for these communities, since most of them live in severe poverty. *Migration Flow* type of companies are businesses with a strong influence of the values of the country of origin, such as family businesses of Jewish, Japanese, Lebanese, German origin, etc., which we have described in this chapter and which open a path for comparative research between Latin American family businesses, for example of the same migratory origin in different regions or in the same region with different migrant origins. It could even be analyzed how, within the same migratory origin, there is a system of cooperation and assistance that promotes the development of the family business. This would increase our knowledge of this type of family business and may shed light on the elements and practices of succession, ownership, and governance of successful family businesses of this type that contribute to this field of knowledge. *Multilatina-type* companies are already consolidated businesses and international family business groups that have taken on a relevant regional and global role, and that contribute with a good part of the wealth of the countries in which they are located. Therefore, further research on their legacy, heritage, and leadership in the family business system can contribute to increase our thoughtful of their practices and dynamics that have led them to this position, as well as to extract the way to share them with family businesses that are in this process of evolution. The Global Entrepreneur type of company, in which innovative business models with global impact are developed, is also a vein to investigate from the perspective of family entrepreneurship, not only from the process of creating new business models, products, and services, but also from the impact and resources offered by the entrepreneurial family. Creating these ventures, from entrepreneurship funds, governance for entrepreneurship, generational dynamics that combine tradition with innovation, etc., is very important because they are the companies that will remain in force in the future and increasing our knowledge of these elements will contribute to this achievement.

Investigating and researching the relationships between these four family business typologies together would allow us to better understand the heterogeneity of family businesses, since it would give us the ability to understand their different ways of being and the characteristics that define them. These four typologies are not necessarily mutually exclusive. For example, a Multilatina may be of Migration Flow origin, or it may be the case that a type of Global Entrepreneur is a product or service of Indigenous Entrepreneurship. It can also happen that a heterogenic typology of family business drives the other: Multilatinas can provoke the development of Indigenous Entrepreneurship or Global Entrepreneur. Similarly, they may evolve from one typology to another; for example, the Global Entrepreneur may evolve into Multilatina. Taking the complete history of a family business from its origins to the present day with a historical and longitudinal perspective in each of these typologies of family business heterogeneity can also be a research opportunity to increase our thoughtful of the characteristics of family businesses in the Latin American region. As it is often said, in historical topics sometimes the biography or narrative of a character or an institution can better reflect and explain the history of a country. Similarly, the narratives and biographies of particular family firms can help to better understand the history of family businesses in Latin America.

This book has presented the importance of taking a step back and observing that family business behaviors have a deeper origin. We recommend that research in this field incorporate other areas of knowledge such as sociology and anthropology in order to explain current phenomena and to be able to recommend best practices especially for the managerial and owner level, bridging theory, and practice.

References

Bizberg, I. (2019). *Diversity of capitalisms in Latin America* (Vol. 49). Palgrave Macmillan.

Carr, J. C., Chrisman, J. J., Chua, J. H., & Steier, L. P. (2016). Family firm challenges in intergenerational wealth transfer. *Entrepreneurship Theory and Practice, 40*(6), 1197–1208. https://doi.org/10.1111/etap.12240.

Colli, A., & Fernández, P. (2013). Business history and family firms. In L. Melin, M. Nordqvist, & P. Sharma. (2013). *Sage handbook of family firms* (pp. 269–292). Londres: Sage.

De Cruz and Jimenez. (2017). Latin American Entrepreneur Families: How to increase cross-generational potential.

Gimeno, A., Baulenas, G., & Coma-Cros, J. (2010). Family business models. In *Family business models* (pp. 57–77). London: Palgrave Macmillan.

Kwon, S. W., & Adler, P. S. (2014). Social capital: Maturation of a field of research. *Academy of Management Review, 39*(4), 412–422.

Latin American STEP Report. (2019). The succession process in Latin American family businesses.

Macpherson, W. G., Tretiakov, A., Mika, J. P., & Felzensztein, C. (2021). Indigenous entrepreneurship: Insights from Chile and New Zealand. *Journal of Business Research, 127,* 77–84.

Moores, K., & Mula, J. (2000). The salience of market, bureaucratic, and clan controls in the management of family firm transitions: Some tentative Australian evidence. *Family Business Review, 13*(2), 91–106.

Index

CPSIA information can be obtained
at www.ICGtesting.com
Printed in the USA
LVHW080800260822
726792LV00008B/178

9 783030 789336